The Duke of Newcastle, 1693–1768, and Henry Pelham, 1694–1754

A Bibliography

Recent Titles in
Bibliographies of British Statesmen

Lord Curzon, 1839–1925: A Bibliography
James G. Parker

Lord Nelson, 1758–1805: A Bibliography
Leonard W. Cowie

The Duke of Wellington, 1769–1852: A Bibliography
Michael Partridge

Charles James Fox, 1749–1806: A Bibliography
David Schweitzer

George Grenville, 1712–1770: A Bibliography
Rory T. Cornish

William Wilberforce, 1759–1833: A Bibliography
Leonard W. Cowie

Margaret Thatcher: A Bibliography
Faysal Mikdadi

William Pitt, Earl of Chatham, 1708–1778: A Bibliography
Karl W. Schweizer

Lord Palmerston, 1784–1865: A Bibliography
Michael S. Partridge and Karen E. Partridge

Edmund Burke, 1729–1797: A Bibliography
Leonard W. Cowie

Sir Robert Peel, 1788–1850: A Bibliography
Leonard W. Cowie

The Duke of Newcastle, 1693–1768, and Henry Pelham, 1694–1754

A Bibliography

P. J. Kulisheck

BIBLIOGRAPHIES OF
BRITISH STATESMEN, NUMBER 8
GREGORY PALMER, SERIES EDITOR

Greenwood Press
Westport, Connecticut • London

Library of Congress Cataloging-in-Publication Data

Kulisheck, P. J., 1937–
    The Duke of Newcastle, 1693–1768, and Henry Pelham, 1694–1754 : a
bibliography / P. J. Kulisheck.
       p.   cm.—(Bibliographies of British statesmen, ISSN
1056–5515 ; no. 8)
    Includes indexes.
    ISBN 0–313–29501–8 (alk. paper)
    1. Newcastle, Thomas Pelham-Holles, Duke of, 1693–1768—
Bibliography.   2. Great Britain—Politics and government—18th
century—Bibliography.   3. Statesmen—Great Britain—Biography—
Bibliography.   4. Pelham, Henry, 1695?–1754—Bibliography.
I. Title. II. Series.
Z8621.5.K85   1997
[DA501.N5]
016.94107′2′092—dc21   97–22561

British Library Cataloguing in Publication Data is available.

Library of Congress Catalog Card Number: 97–22561
ISBN: 0–313–29501–8
ISSN: 1056–5515

First published in 1997

Greenwood Press, 88 Post Road West, Westport, CT 06881
An imprint of Greenwood Publishing Group, Inc.

Printed in the United States of America

∞™

The paper used in this book complies with the
Permanent Paper Standard issued by the National
Information Standards Organization (Z39.48–1984).

10 9 8 7 6 5 4 3 2 1

His Grace the late worthy Duke of Newcastle, among his other good and amiable Qualities, was likewise a sagacious and consummate Politician: he kept copies of all the Letters he sent to foreign Courts, and constantly preserved all the original Letters which he received in return: and in the year 1744, when this Kingdom was threatened with a French Invasion, and in 1745, when an actual Rebellion broke out, he had better Intelligence than ever the famous Thurloe, Secretary to Oliver Cromwell, had, during the Government of that great and successful usurper....

Whitehall Evening Post, 3 December 1768

Mr. Pelham died in March 1754, and our Tranquility, both at home and abroad, expired with him. He had acquired the Reputation of an able, and honest Minister, had a plain, solid Understanding, improved by Experience in Business, as well as by a thorough knowledge of the World; and without being an Orator, or having the finest Parts, no Man in the House of Commons argued with more Weight, or was heard with greater attention. He was a frugal Steward to the Public, averse to continental Extravagance, and useless Subsidies; preferring a tolerable Peace to the most successful War; jealous to maintain his personal Credit, and authority; but nowise inattentive to the true Interest of his Country.

James Waldegrave, 2nd Earl Waldegrave, 1758

The Duke of Newcastle. Portrait c. 1750 by William Hoare. Engraved by James McArdell.
© Crown copyright: UK Government Art Collection.

Henry Pelham. Portrait c. 1750, possibly by John Giles Eccardt. © Crown copyright: UK Government Art Collection.

Contents

PREFACE   xi

INTRODUCTION   xiii

CHRONOLOGY OF SIGNIFICANT EVENTS IN THE
LIVES OF THE PELHAM BROTHERS   xix

1. UNPUBLISHED PERSONAL PAPERS   1

    A. Great Britain   1

    B. Canada   29

    C. Jamaica   29

    D. United States   29

2. PUBLISHED COMPILATIONS OF ORIGINAL PAPERS
CONTAINING PELHAM BROTHERS' LETTERS   35

    A. Historical Manuscripts Commission Reports   35

    B. Other Collections   38

3. CONTEMPORARY MEMOIRS, DIARIES, AND
CORRESPONDENCE CONTAINING IMPORTANT
MATERIAL ON THE PELHAMS   45

4. SPEECHES IN PARLIAMENT   51

5. PAMPHLETS RELATING TO THE PELHAMS   55

6. NEWSPAPERS   59

7. JOURNALS AND PERIODICALS   63

8. THE PELHAMS' LIVES AND CAREERS   65

    A. Biographies   65

    B. Early Life, Family, and Genealogy   67

    C. Early Careers   68

    D. Pelham as Chief Minister   73

    E. Newcastle as Secretary of State   80

    F. Newcastle at the Treasury   89

    G. Newcastle's Last Years   92

9. SPECIAL TOPICS   95

    A. Newcastle's Ecclesiastical Patronage   95

    B. The Pelhams and America   98

    C. The War of the Austrian Succession   99

    D. The Seven Years War   102

10. PORTRAITS, SATIRES, AND POEMS   107

11. PLACES ASSOCIATED WITH THE PELHAMS   113

12. IDEOLOGY AND HISTORIOGRAPHY   115

13. BIBLIOGRAPHIES AND GUIDES TO FURTHER
    MATERIALS   119

14. RECENT HISTORIES OF EIGHTEENTH-CENTURY
    BRITAIN   123

INDEX TO AUTHORS   125

INDEX TO CORRESPONDENTS AND SUBJECTS   131

Preface

This bibliography provides a variety of sources relating to the lives and careers of the Pelham brothers, who, because of their long service to the Crown, played such a prominent role in public affairs in mid-eighteenth-century Britain. The correspondence of the Duke of Newcastle, because of the great quantity of it preserved in the British Library and Public Record Office, has long been the first resort of researchers studying politics and governmental administration. While not definitive, this volume does cover that well-known material, other manuscripts, and printed primary and secondary sources selected and arranged to assist further research. The material included centers on the Pelhams or provides important commentary on them or their era and is arranged by type or topic. Each chapter includes an introduction and annotated entries. Because manuscripts usually can be used only in the repositories holding them, Chapter 1 is arranged geographically, the bulk of manuscripts being held in Great Britain. In Chapter 2 (printed letters), the Historical Manuscripts Commission Reports are listed in their usual order of citation and the other collections are listed roughly chronologically, that is, those relevant to the Pelhams' early years are listed first. Works in Chapters 3 and 5 also are listed chronologically, although the influential writings of Horace Walpole open Chapter 3. The works within the subdivisions of Chapters 8 and 9 are grouped by topic and, where possible, chronologically within the topic. Chapters 4, 6, and 7 list primary sources first and then reference works and studies. Chapters 10-14 are arranged in the order that seems most useful for research on the topic covered. The names of relevant reference works are included where appropriate. Special attention has been paid to the needs of researchers who live outside the United Kingdom, those who must depend on Interlibrary Loan, and those who work independently.

While thanks are due to the staffs of many record offices and archives for their assistance in gathering material for this volume, I must mention in particular the exceptional effort made by the staff of the National Register of Archives and Roger Golding and David Law of the Government Art Collection.

The University of Minnesota Libraries' excellent staff and extensive collection of works on eighteenth-century British history eased the burden of my research. I thank Cynthia Harris, executive editor, academic reference books, at Greenwood Press for her advice and patience. My husband Richard provided the technical expertise and moral support needed to complete this book.

Introduction

The Pelham brothers' importance in British history has been confirmed only in the last half of this century. Henry Pelham long was seen as the dull but honest successor to the brilliant Sir Robert Walpole. His brother Thomas, Duke of Newcastle, often was taken at Horace Walpole's estimation: a garrulous fool who somehow was still crafty enough to gain the highest offices. Yet the Pelhams successfully guided Britain through a rebellion and two great wars. Examining these events has caused historians to look past Newcastle's eccentricities to see the tireless worker devoted to his country's welfare and prestige. As Brewer has shown, Pelham was an able administrator whose financial reforms enabled Britain to survive the drains of the Seven Years War. Pelham reduced "the size of the fiscal bureaucracy," and his "rescheduling of the redeemable debt...was the major fiscal achievement of mid-century."[1]

Advancements in technology and archival organization have allowed historians to sift out from the mass of sources a much clearer picture of the possibilities and constraints under which the Pelhams operated. Government was still departmental, like the American executive branch, with each head responsible directly to a King who was keenly interested and involved in the direction of affairs. Although Pelham nominally became chief minister when appointed First Lord of the Treasury in 1743, he needed several years to secure his position in Commons and win the King's confidence, thus becoming minister for the King in Commons and minister for Commons "in the Closet." As Owen points out, Pelham was chief minister "because he had to defend the *whole* of the Administration's policy" in Commons.[2] Certainly Newcastle's being a Secretary of State gave Pelham unusual opportunities to offer advice on the conduct of foreign affairs and also, on occasion, to offend his touchy brother. Pelham's job was in one way the easier in that George II interfered little in the operations of the Treasury or in domestic affairs in Commons. Newcastle had to trim his policies to suit the King and could not expect foreign ministers to be as cooperative as the Whig majority in Parliament.

Born into a family that espoused the Whig cause and Revolution principles, the Pelham brothers served the House of Hanover all their adult lives, out of their belief that certain policies must be implemented. Conviction, however, was joined to need. A rich man, Newcastle nevertheless needed work to give his life meaning: "...my natural love of politics, and being concerned in the public world, both in town and country, will make a private life very disagreeable to me."[3] Pelham needed an income because he was a younger son. For an intelligent and ambitious man of his birth, a seat in Commons opened the prospect of a salaried post in the ministry, followed by higher office and, perhaps, the reward of a peerage.

Thomas Pelham was born on 21 July 1693, and his only surviving brother Henry, on 26 September 1694.[4] They were the sons of Sir Thomas Pelham of Laughton, Sussex, and his second wife Lady Grace, sister of John Holles, Duke of Newcastle. Sir Thomas was the fourth Pelham baronet to both sit in Commons and marry well, and in 1706 he was created Baron Pelham. Lady Grace died in 1700. The brothers attended Westminster School and then went on to university: Thomas to Clare Hall, Cambridge, and Henry to Hart Hall, Oxford. This must have been the first prolonged separation of brothers only fourteen months apart in age. In later life, this closeness in age was reflected in their great mutual affection and their deeply felt quarrels. The difference in their expectations increased abruptly in 1711, when Newcastle died, leaving the bulk of his great estate to his nephew Thomas, provided he added the name Holles. Thomas inherited another substantial estate from his father in 1712. The new Baron Pelham, barely twenty years old, had an income of about £25,000 a year, making him one of the richest men in the country. When Henry married Lady Katherine Manners in 1726, his brother gave him part of the Pelham estate to provide a suitable income. Thomas himself married Lady Henrietta Godolphin, granddaughter of the 1st Duke of Marlborough, in 1717.

Following family tradition, Pelham-Holles threw himself into Whig politics in 1713, helping found a club supporting the Hanoverian Succession. This devotion earned him the title Earl of Clare on the accession of George I in 1714. The following year, while his brother Henry served as a volunteer, Clare raised a troop of soldiers to fight the Pretender and in reward was made Duke of Newcastle. The brothers entered government in 1717, when Newcastle was appointed Lord Chamberlain and Pelham was elected to Commons for Seaford, Sussex. Although the brothers would thereafter work as a team until Pelham's death, their political experiences would differ. Newcastle sat in the House of Lords and attended at Court first as Chamberlain and then as Secretary of State for the Southern Department from 1724. Pelham soon gained favor with Sir Robert Walpole, who brought him to the Treasury Board in 1721 and obtained his promotion to Secretary at War in 1724 and Paymaster General in 1730. As a Secretary, Newcastle looked outward, to relations with the continental powers and the colonies, and concerned himself with implementing the monarch's directives on policy. As Walpole's lieutenant in Commons, Pelham looked inward, mastering the financial structure that supported the monarch's policy and learning how to extract support for his measures from the members of Commons and thus the country. As Secretary at War and Paymaster, he saw just how much military defense of foreign policy could cost. Pelham also learned from Walpole how to ensure a majority vote in Commons for his measures by securing government jobs for supporters and managing elections. This difference in experience and responsibilities was the chief source of friction between the brothers when they headed their administration. They differed even in appearance and personality. Newcastle, thin and fidgety, irritated colleagues with his talkativeness and touchy sensibility. Pelham, growing ever plumper, usually was calm in temper and skillful in persuading colleagues to work in harmony.

Newcastle inherited local electoral influence along with his great estates, which allowed him to get Pelham seated first for Seaford and then in 1722 for the county of Sussex. The Duke also found a seat in 1719 for a young attorney named Philip Yorke, who became Newcastle's confidant and, after Pelham's death, chief adviser. Yorke rose with the Pelhams, becoming Lord Chancellor and Earl of Hardwicke. The extent of Newcastle's electoral influence was much conjectured by both his contemporaries and historians. Owen found the Duke "could never in his private capacity return more than nine members (frequently only seven)", a great number for one man but few compared to the forty to sixty-five controlled by the government.[5] Contemporaries also believed that Newcastle, despite his great income, was badly in debt throughout his life because he spent too much on electioneering. After studying the Duke's accounts, Kelch concluded Newcastle's lavish life-style and construction costs of his country home Claremont ate up his income and that he needed his large salaries from office to survive.[6] These debts were another source of conflict between the brothers because Newcastle was childless and his estate would devolve upon Pelham or his children. Pelham also worried about the threat to his brother's good name and credit and to the estate itself if land had to be sold to meet debts.

As Lord Chamberlain, Newcastle was a member of the Privy Council and reported directly to the King. He owed his appointment to Charles Spencer, 3rd Earl of Sunderland, but, after the collapse of the latter's ministry over the South Sea Company scandal and his death in 1722, Newcastle allied himself with Walpole and Charles Townshend, 2nd Viscount Townshend, respectively First Lord of the Treasury and Secretary of State for the Northern Department. The Duke so ably assisted these two in their power struggle with John Carteret, Baron Carteret, that he himself was appointed to replace the latter as Southern Secretary in April 1724. At the same time, Pelham, who was now close enough to Walpole to be a frequent guest at Houghton, was appointed Secretary at War. The brothers had risen rapidly in government, partly by ability and partly by

Newcastle's liberal spending in the Whig cause.

Over the next ten years, the Pelhams understudied their eventual roles. Walpole, intent on peace that kept the land tax low and Commons tractable, became increasingly dissatisfied with Townshend's conduct of foreign affairs and was able to exert more influence on foreign policy after the Secretary, ill and exhausted, resigned in 1730. That same year Pelham became Paymaster General, potentially a most lucrative post, which he refused to exploit. Walpole's dominance created opposition, and, when it first came to a head in the Excise Crisis in 1733, the Pelhams provided loyal support. By 1739, however, Newcastle disagreed with the "Great Man" on the question of war with Spain. Clamor outdoors and within Commons forced Walpole into a war for which Britain, and especially its navy, was not properly prepared and then forced him from office in 1742 because the war went badly. The Pelhams' apprenticeship was over.

The brothers remained in their offices during the complex negotiations over a new administration, which Owen so carefully reconstructed. Advised by Walpole, now Lord Orford, Pelham first agreed to attend the Cabinet as minister for Commons and, in 1743, to become First Lord of the Treasury and Chancellor of the Exchequer. Carteret, now Northern Secretary, held the Pelhams in contempt, had the King's ear, and did not understand why he needed Commons too. Of Newcastle Owen writes: "Made to appear ridiculous by his strange external eccentricities, and subject always to a host of neurotic fears and jealousies, he was physically and temperamentally ill equipped for the strenuous demands of statesmanship," but none can read his papers "without being impressed by his comprehensive knowledge of foreign politics, his cogent and consistently-held principles, and his ample fund of shrewd common sense."[7] Newcastle believed Carteret's policies for conducting the war were wrong and, with the assistance of his brother and Hardwicke, forced his resignation in 1744. Finding Carteret still exerted influence without office, the Pelhams, together with most members of the ministry, resigned on 10 and 11 February. Their control of a majority in Parliament prevented the formation of a new ministry, and they returned to office on 13 February, to serve an angry monarch.

Having secured the promise of the King's confidence, the Pelhams set about gaining his trust. A snap general election in 1747 gave Pelham a solid base in Commons. The peace signed in 1748 was inconclusive but quieted domestic opposition. Although disaffected politicians were drawn to a party formed by the Prince of Wales, his death in 1751 turned them back to the Pelhams. Newcastle used the peacetime to form alliances he believed would again be needed to counter France, quarreling with his brother over the use of subsidies to gain support. Pelham turned to domestic issues, overseeing bills designed to redress grievances over questions of social welfare. Pelham pleased the King by cutting the debts of the Civil List. He also began work on a plan to gradually lower the rate of interest on the national debt from four to three percent. This reduction, together with consolidation of the debt, was Pelham's great legacy to the nation and his brother. The support Pelham earned from King and Commons made him chief minister but also made Newcastle jealous despite his great love for his brother. The Duke channeled some of his frustration into becoming George II's chief advisor on foreign policy, persuading the King first to make him Northern Secretary in 1748 and then to replace the independent Bedford with the pliable Holdernesse in 1751.

Although he had been unwell for about a year, Pelhams's death on 6 March 1754 was unexpected. He was mourned by many, in particular the old King, who said he would now have no more peace. Hardwicke persuaded George II and the Council that Newcastle should succeed his brother, even though he had no experience in that branch of government and could not manage Commons from inside. Yet Newcastle grew in office, becoming a very capable First Lord of the Treasury. Soon after the Duke had secured a solid majority in the 1754 general election, strained relations with France in North America flared into open conflict, leading Britain to declare war in 1756. Newcastle was blamed for the loss of Minorca that year and the resulting execution of Admiral Byng. On the latter, at least, he probably had no choice, with the King and the mob determined on death.

The problem of Commons was never solved and gave William Pitt a foothold into real influence in 1756 and coalition with Newcastle in 1757. While this coalition won the war because capable and energetic men headed all the important departments of government, Newcastle's ability to raise unprecedented sums of money was a key factor.[8] When the prospect of peace made the Duke no longer necessary, he was maneuvered out of office, but not out of politics, by George III in 1762. Newcastle, for the first time in his life, went into opposition, supporting the Rockingham Whigs. Even after suffering a slight stroke in December 1767, Newcastle remained active in Sussex politics until shortly before his death in November 1768.

The Pelham brothers appear to have believed in their family motto, which placed love of country above all else. They served that country during the period in which it became the greatest power in Europe. Whether other men might have served her as well or better is unknowable. That either brother could have succeeded alone is unlikely.

NOTES

1. John Brewer, *The Sinews of Power: War, Money and the English State, 1688-1783* (New York: Knopf, 1989), pp. 87 and 124.

2. John B. Owen, *The Rise of the Pelhams* (London: Methuen, 1957), p. 319.

3. Newcastle in a letter to Pelham 2 October 1741, printed in William Coxe, *Memoirs of the Administration of the Right Honourable Henry Pelham* (London: Longman, 1829, 2 vols.), v.1, p. 23.

4. Newcastle's birthdate is well documented, but Pelham's has been unknown. Janet Seaton found this date for Pelham in v.1, p. 351, of Alexander Jacob's *A Complete English Peerage* (London: Printed by the Author and sold by J. Wilson, 1766-1767, 2 vols.). An accompanying genealogical table gives the date as 25 September, possibly a typographical error. Confirmation of the year can be found in the wording of the plate on Pelham's coffin, as given by L. B. Smith in "The Pelham Vault" (*The Sussex County Magazine* 4 (1930): 370-372), p. 371. Pelham died 6 March 1754 "in the 60th year of his age," that is, between the fifty-ninth and sixtieth anniversaries of his birth.

5. J. B. Owen, "Political Patronage in 18th Century England" in Paul Fritz and David Williams, eds., *The Triumph of Culture: 18th Century Perspectives* (Toronto: Hakkert, 1972), pp. 369-387; quote p. 377.

6. Ray Kelch, *Newcastle, A Duke Without Money: Thomas Pelham-Holles, 1693-1768* (Berkeley: University of California Press, 1974), pp. 195-207.

7. Owen, *The Rise of the Pelhams*, p. 128.

8. Richard Middleton, *The Bells of Victory: The Pitt-Newcastle Ministry and the Conduct of the Seven Years' War, 1757-1762* (Cambridge: Cambridge University Press, 1985).

Chronology of Significant Events in the Lives of the Pelham Brothers

1693	21	July	Thomas Pelham born in London, son of Sir Thomas Pelham and his second wife Lady Grace Holles, daughter of Gilbert, 3rd Earl of Clare.
1694	26	September	Henry Pelham born, possibly in London.
1699?			Thomas enters Westminster School, London.
1700?			Henry enters Westminster School.
	13	September	Lady Grace Pelham dies, leaving six daughters and two sons.
1709	9	May	Thomas admitted to Clare Hall, Cambridge.
1710	6	September	Henry enters Hart Hall, Oxford.
1711	15	July	Thomas adds Holles to his name upon inheriting estates of uncle John Holles, Duke of Newcastle.
1712	23	February	Sir Thomas (now Baron Pelham) dies.
1714		August	Accession of George I.
	19	October	Lord Pelham created Earl of Clare.
1715	22	July	Henry volunteers to fight Jacobite rebellion.
	11	August	Clare created Duke of Newcastle-upon-Tyne. Henry begins a tour of the Continent.

1717	28	February	Pelham elected M.P. for Seaford, Sussex, while still on tour.
	2	April	Newcastle weds Lady Harriet Godolphin, grand-daughter of the 1st Duke of Marlborough.
	13	April	Newcastle appointed Lord Chamberlain of the Royal Household and a Privy Councillor.
		October	Pelham returns from the Continent.
1720	25	May	Pelham appointed Treasurer of the Chamber for George, Prince of Wales.
1721	3	April	Pelham appointed a member of the Treasury Board.
1722		March	Pelham elected M.P. for Sussex.
1724	3	April	Pelham appointed Secretary at War.
	14	April	Newcastle appointed Secretary of State for the Southern Department.
1725	1	June	Pelham appointed a Privy Councillor.
1726	29	October	Pelham marries Lady Katherine Manners, daughter of the 2nd Duke of Rutland, who bore him two sons and six daughters.
1727		June	Accession of George II.
1730	8	May	Pelham appointed Paymaster General.
1739	19	October	War with Spain begins.
	27-28	November	Death of Pelham's sons Henry and Thomas at ages 10 and 3 from a throat infection.
1740	20	October	Maria Theresa succeeds to the throne of Austria.
	16	December	Frederick II of Prussia seizes Silesia, opening the War of the Austrian Succession.
1741	8	April	Parliament approves British support of Austria against Prussia and France.
		October	Newcastle considers resigning over a policy dispute with Walpole but is dissuaded by Pelham and Hardwicke.

1742	11 February	Sir Robert Walpole resigns.
	16 February	Earl of Wilmington named First Lord of Treasury, with Carteret and Newcastle as Secretaries of State.
1743	16 June	George II leads troops at victory of Dettingen.
	2 July	Death of Wilmington.
	25 August	Pelham appointed First Lord of the Treasury.
	12 December	Pelham made Chancellor of the Exchequer.
1744	29 March	Britain declares war on France.
	24 November	Pelham brothers force resignation of Carteret.
1745	8 January	Formation of Quadruple Alliance.
	25 July	Outbreak of second Jacobite Rebellion.
1746	11 February	Pelhams resign, resume office three days later after Bath and Carteret fail to form a ministry.
	16 April	Battle of Culloden ends the Jacobite Rebellion.
1747	20 June	Snap election brings Pelham an increased majority in Commons.
1748	6 February	Newcastle becomes Secretary of State for the Northern Department.
	7 October	Treaty of Aix-la-Chapelle ends the War of the Austrian Succession.
1751	20 March	Death of Frederick, Prince of Wales.
	14 June	Newcastle persuades George II to dismiss Sandwich from the Admiralty, forcing Bedford's resignation as Southern Secretary.
1754	6 March	Pelham dies in London and is buried at Laughton.
	16 March	Newcastle appointed First Lord of the Treasury.
	July	Armed conflict with France flares up in America.
1756	16 January	Treaty of Westminster with Prussia signed.
	18 May	Britain declares war on France, beginning the Seven Years War.
	11 November	Newcastle resigns in the face of opposition over his conduct of the war.

1757	29	June	Newcastle returns to the Treasury in coalition with Pitt as Southern Secretary of State.
	26	July	French occupy Hanover.
1758	11	April	British subsidy treaty with Prussia guarantees needed support in war.
1759			*Annus mirabilis* of British naval and military victories.
1760	31	July	Hanover recovered from French control.
	25	October	Death of George II. New young King determined to change policies and ministers.
1761		March	Bute appointed Northern Secretary.
	5	October	Pitt resigns over question of war with Spain.
1762	26	May	Newcastle resigns over policy differences with Bute and Grenville.
1764	6	March	Death of Lord Hardwicke.
1765	15	July	Newcastle appointed Lord Privy Seal in the Rockingham Administration.
1766	30	July	Newcastle leaves office for the last time.
1768	17	November	Newcastle dies in London and is buried at Laughton in the family tomb.

1

Unpublished Personal Papers

A. GREAT BRITAIN

A searchable electronic database at the National Register of Archives, Quality House, Quality Court, Chancery Lane, London WC2A 1HP, lists names of correspondents and location of letters. It can be accessed at http://www.hmc. gov.uk/ or telnet public.hmc.gov.uk. E-mail can be sent to nra@hmc.gov.uk. NRA has catalogues of most collections in public and private hands and can provide information about access. These catalogues vary, with some giving only general listings and others detailing each item. Enquiries about fees and conditions of use should be sent to the manuscripts' owners. The *National Inventory of Documentary Sources in the United Kingdom and Ireland*, a microfiche index of many but not all collections published by Chadwyck-Healey Ltd., is available in some larger university libraries. An index to *NIDS* has been issued on CD-ROM. Locations of manuscript collections included in the printed Reports of the Royal Commission on Historical Manuscripts (HMC) are published in the Commission's *Guide to the Locations of Collections Described in the Reports and Calendar Series 1870-1980* (London: HMSO, 1982). All locations should be verified because collections change hands with some frequency. Addresses and guides to collections are listed in *British Archives* by Janet Foster and Julia Sheppard (New York: Stockton Press, 1995, 3rd ed.) and in *Record Repositories in Great Britain* issued by the HMC (London: HMSO, 1992, 9th ed.). The *Index of Manuscripts in the British Library* (Cambridge: Chadwyck-Healey, 1984, 10 vols.) reproduces the person and place entries, including volume and folio number, from 22 *Catalogues of Additions* published between 1843 and 1979. Users should study the introduction in v. 1. Manuscripts increasingly are being copied on microfilm or microfiche to preserve the originals and make them more accessible. Some are listed in this volume, but new issues should be sought in the latest edition of *Guide to Microforms in Print* (Munich: Saur, 1996), a four-volume set, two each of author-title and subject (look under Great Britain). The Center for Research Libraries, Chicago, owns many microforms and loans them to its member libraries in the United States and Canada. In New Zealand, the Alexander Turnbull Library, Wellington, is a possible source, and in Australia, the Melbourne University Library. In the United Kingdom, the British Library Document Supply Centre, Boston Spa, provides interlibrary loans.

British Library Department of Manuscripts, Great Russell Street, London WC1B 3DG (until mid-1998).

This collection will move to the new British Library, 96 Euston Road, London NW1 2DB, in the summer of 1998. In consequence, the collection will be closed to all use and enquiries for at least August-December 1998. Updated information about the Library's move to St. Pancras can be found at http://www.bl.uk/. Questions about the Manuscripts Department closure can be directed by e-mail to mss@bl.uk or by post to the Great Russell Street address. To compensate for the closure, this *Bibliography* includes full information on the published catalogues, which are held by many larger libraries. (The Manuscript Room copies are annotated with additions and corrections.) *The British Library: Guide to the Catalogues and Indexes of the Department of Manuscripts* by M.A.E. Nickson (London: British Library, 1982, 2nd ed.) is no longer accurate and was revised in 1996 by Julian Conway. The revision is available in the Manuscripts Room and will be published, probably in 1998.

1.   Newcastle Papers: Additional Manuscripts 32686-33083. Newcastle's correspondence, bound in 307 volumes, forms the major part of this collection, which is listed (pp. 235-257) and indexed in *Catalogue of Additions to the Manuscripts in the British Museum in the Years 1882-1887* (London: Museum Trustees, 1889). Both in-letters and fair copies of the Duke's out-letters are bound in roughly chronological order, providing easy access to both sides of correspondence. Researchers use these copies in place of lost original letters and for comparison with surviving letters in other collections because Newcastle's handwriting became increasingly indecipherable over time. The Papers cover every aspect of the Duke's public and private life, including his political and official activities, correspondence with his wife, his personal income and expenses, his estates, even the menus of his lavish dinners. Individuals' index entries usually include their letters both to and from Newcastle, although the latter are not designated as such. Some letters were omitted from the index by accident, and some are bound out of order in volumes for the wrong year. Notes written into the mountings of the folios point out these errors. These corrections, unfortunately, are not included in the microfilm listed below.

     a. Pelham's letters (c. 200) to his brother (indexed pp. 896-897) are scattered throughout the collection and are most numerous in the years the Duke visited Hanover (1748, 1750, and 1752). Pelham's papers (66) include some copies of letters he wrote.

b. Volumes 32686-32737 and 32852-329992 (general and home correspondence) have been microfilmed by Harvester as *Papers of the Prime Ministers of Great Britain, Series Four: The Papers of The Duke of Newcastle.* This set of 185 reels is divided into ten parts and may be borrowed through Interlibrary Loan (by part only) from the Center for Research Libraries, Chicago. It also is available in the Manuscripts Room as Microfilm 932, 936, 941, 948, 954, 970, 1008, and 1014.

> Part 1: 32686-32701 (1697-1743).
> Part 2: 32702-32719 (1744-1749).
> Part 3: 32720-32737 (1750-1754).
> Part 4: 32852-32869 (1755-1756).
> Part 5: 32870-32886 (1757-1758).
> Part 6: 32887-32907 (1759-June 1760).
> Part 7: 32908-32932 (July 1760-1761).
> Part 8: 32933-32954 (1762-1763).
> Part 9: 32955-32972 (1764-1765).
> Part 10: 32973-32992 (1766-1768).

Overlooked items 1741-1768 are bound in 32991B, and undated letters, in 32992. The dates of the individual volumes are listed in the *Catalogue*, pp. 239-241 and 245-250.

c. 33003: Letters from Newcastle to John White concerning changes in the ministry June 1765-Oct 1767 (*Catalogue*, p. 251). See Bateson (189) and McCahill (397).

d. 32684: Letters from members of Royal Family 1732-1768, mostly to Newcastle (*Catalogue*, pp. 237-238).

e. 32685: Letters 1714-1761 to Pelham and Newcastle from notable men, chiefly authors and playwrights (*Catalogue*, pp. 238-239).

f. 33198-33201: Correspondence and papers concerning Coxe's *Pelham Administration* and Earl of Chichester's draft edition of Newcastle's letters, with transcripts from Newcastle Papers (*Catalogue*, pp. 268-269).

g. 33344: Miscellaneous Newcastle Papers 1685-1752, chiefly parliamentary, diplomatic, and official (*Catalogue*, p. 296).

h. 32993-33002: Miscellaneous papers 1667-1768, including drafts, notes for speeches, minutes of Cabinet meetings; 33004: Minutes of Cabinet meetings 1739-1745 (*Catalogue*, p. 251).

i. 33033-33037: Papers of proceedings in Parliament 1689-1768, (*Catalogue*, p. 252).

j. 33038-33041: Miscellaneous papers relating to taxation and finance 1688-1803, including Newcastle's official papers. (*Catalogue*, p. 252).

k. 33042: Book of fees and forms for official documents; includes list of expenses 1733-1740 for such things as assizes and proclamations (*Catalogue*, p. 252).

l. 33043: List of Customs officers and their salaries 1761; 33044: List of salaries and pensions 1754-1762 (*Catalogue*, p. 252).

m. 33045: Papers relating to the Royal household 1600s-1774, mainly Newcastle's official papers (*Catalogue*, p. 253).

n. 33051-33053: Miscellaneous papers relating to government 1262-1783, including Acts of Parliament, patents for inventions, and revenue schemes (*Catalogue*, pp. 254-256).

o. 33054-33057: Miscellaneous papers, mainly petitions and memorials received by Newcastle (*Catalogue*, p. 256).

Newcastle's 30 years as Secretary of State generated many volumes of documents. These are not available on microfilm. See also his letters to Pelham on foreign affairs in (66).

p. 32738-32851: Diplomatic correspondence 1724-1754 (*Catalogue*, pp. 241-245).

q. 33005-33025: Papers concerning foreign affairs or negotiations with foreign countries 1602-1767; 33026-33027: Despatches from envoys to Paris 1749-1754 (*Catalogue*, pp. 251-252).

r. 33028-33030: Papers concerning the American and West Indian colonies 1701-1802; 33031: Papers concerning the East India Company 1695-1802; 33032: Papers concerning the South Sea Company 1710-1753 (*Catalogue*, p. 252).

s. 33046-33048: Papers concerning the Army and Navy 1600s-1803 (*Catalogue*, p. 253).

t. 33049: Papers concerning Scotland 1715-1802, mainly fiscal, political, or official; 33050: Papers concerning Scottish Jacobites 1745-1755 (*Catalogue*, p. 253).

Documents relating to Newcastle's family, estates, and local political influence make up a large portion of his papers.

u. 33062: Newcastle's memorandum book, mostly rough notes; 33063: Patents of honors and appointments conferred on Newcastle 1714-1765 (*Catalogue*, p. 256).

v. 33073-33078: Correspondence between the Duke and his wife Henrietta (Harriet) 1714-1768; 33064-33072: Newcastle's private correspondence 1711-1768, including letters to Duchess and his agents; 33082-33083: Duchess of Newcastle's correspondence 1768-1776; 33079-33080: Letters of Francis Godolphin, 2nd Earl of Godolphin, to his daughter the Duchess 1723-1762 (*Catalogue*, pp. 256-257).

w. 32679: Newcastle's correspondence 1715-1722 with Godolphin (ff. 55-57) and John and Sarah Churchill, Duke and Duchess of Marlborough (ff. 19, 25, 27, 33, 35, 41, 45, 47, 53, 60, 62, 64, 66) (*Catalogue*, pp. 236-237).

x. 33084: Correspondence (ff. 171-187) between 1st Baron Pelham and his brother Henry 1703-1707 about property settlements; 33087: Newcastle correspondence (ff. 309, 334, 368) with his cousin Thomas Pelham of Stanmer 1754-1758; 33088: correspondence with Pelham 1761-1768 about Sussex politics (ff. 20, 67, 81, 104, 110, 112) and Newcastle's final illness and death (f. 119 onward) including three (ff. 174, 178, 195) from the Duke (*Catalogue*, p. 258).

y. 33157: Accounts of agent for Newcastle's property in Sussex 1742-1752; 33158-33160: Newcastle's household expenses 1742-1768; 33162-33163: Newcastle's personal expenses 1744-1753; 33164-33166 and 33168-33169: Rent records from Newcastle's various estates (*Catalogue*, pp. 265-266).

z. 33320, 33323-33324, and 33338: Stewards' accounts for Newcastle's various properties 1725-1769; 33321: Agent's account of Newcastle's receipts and expenses 1737-1754; 33322: Payment of debts records of trustees of Newcastle's estate 1738-1751; 33325-33336: Records and prices of food served in Newcastle's household 1761-1774; 33337: Valuation of furniture in Newcastle's houses 1768-1769 (*Catalogue*, pp. 295-296).

aa. 33167: Records of Pelham's estates in Sussex 1762-1776 (*Catalogue*, p. 266).

bb. 33058-33059: Papers concerning local affairs in Sussex 1581-1814; 33060: Papers concerning Nottinghamshire 1701-1768, chiefly Newcastle as Lord Lieutenant and as Warden of Sherwood Forest; 33061: Papers concerning various local matters 1574-1787, including the Universities of Cambridge (of which Newcastle was Chancellor) and Oxford and the

Charterhouse of London (*Catalogue*, p. 256).

cc. The British Library Additional Charters also include items relating to the Pelham brothers. Add. Ch. 29267-29477: Documents connected with the personal and political life of the Pelham family; 29478-29503: Wills of the Pelham family to 1729; 30988-31065: Court, hundred, and rent rolls connected with the political and personal history of the Pelham family (*Catalogue*, pp. 316-317).

2.   Hardwicke Papers: Additional Manuscripts 35349-36278. Philip Yorke, 1st Earl of Hardwicke (Lord Chancellor 1737-1756), was the Pelham brothers' close friend and political ally. The correspondence and papers of the Yorke family are the second major source of information about the lives and careers of the Pelhams. Many references to them can be found in volumes not listed here. These papers are calendared and indexed in *Catalogue of the Additions to the Manuscripts in the British Museum in the Years 1894-1899* (London: Museum Trustees, 1901).

a. 35406-35422: Hardwicke-Newcastle correspondence 1723-1763, including drafts of Hardwicke's letters and copies of Newcastle's letters to other persons; also 35908 on legal questions concerning trade and the American colonies and 36134-36139 on questions of law, both 1720-1733 (*Catalogue*, pp. 280, 372, 410, and 1212-1214). 35352, f. 167, and 35355, f. 233 (p. 275); 35596, f. 426, 35603, f. 36, and 35604, f. 6 (p. 294).

b. 35425: Newcastle letters to Philip Yorke (2nd Earl) 1761-1767 (*Catalogue*, pp. 282 and 1214).

c. 35429: Newcastle letters to Charles Yorke 1756-1768, chiefly about Cambridge University business; also 36223, f. 117 (*Catalogue*, pp. 284 and 414).

d. 35411 and 35413-35414: Newcastle letters (15) to Hugh Valence Jones 1751-1753 (*Catalogue*, pp. 280 and 1213).

e. 35870: Cabinet and Privy Council minutes and secret memoranda 1733-1766; f. 95, Newcastle in 1745 (*Catalogue*, pp. 355-357).

f. 35454-35455: Newcastle letters (8) to Field-Marshal Lord Stair 1742-1743 (*Catalogue*, pp. 289 and 1212).

g. 35461-35479 and 35483-35484: Newcastle letters 1748-1761 to Robert Keith, envoy at Vienna and St. Petersburg, with copies of the Duke's letters to others (*Catalogue*, pp. 290 and 1213).

h. 35423: Pelham letters (ff. 3-171) to Hardwicke 1724-1754; also

35603, f. 242, and 36134-36137, 13 letters (*Catalogue*, pp. 281, 294, 410, and 1211).

i. 35409-35413 and 35423: Copies of Pelham letters to Newcastle 1748-1752 (*Catalogue*, pp. 280-281 and 1211).

j. 35453-35455: Pelham letters (12) to Lord Stair 1742-1743 (*Catalogue*, pp. 289 and 1211)

k. 35424: Pelham letters (ff. 7-8) to Philip Yorke 1743 and 1747; also 35606, ff. 15 and 83, and 35607, f. 198 (*Catalogue*, p. 281 and 295).

l. 35468: Pelham letters to Robert Keith 1750 (f. 223) and 1751 (35471, f. 65) (*Catalogue*, p. 290).

m. 35351-35372, 35374-35376, 35385, and 35387-35389: Correspondence between Hardwicke, his wife, and their children (*Catalogue*, pp. 275-278).

n. 35895: Papers relating to Admiral John Byng and the loss of Minorca 1756-1757 (*Catalogue*, pp. 366-367).

o. 35337: Parliamentary journal of Philip Yorke (2nd Earl) for 1743-1745 (*Catalogue*, p. 267), showing Pelham as Leader of Commons. Fair copy in Add. MS 9198, f. 47 onward. See Connors (213)

p. 35428: Papers of 2nd Earl concerning political affairs in 1760s (*Catalogue*, pp. 283-284).

The following papers are only indexed in *Index to the Additional Manuscripts, with Those of the Egerton Collection, Preserved in the British Museum, and Acquired in the Years 1783-1835* (London: Museum Trustees, 1966 reprint). The only catalogues are held in the Manuscripts Room.

3. 5827: Newspaper report (ff. 211v-213v) of Newcastle's presiding at Cambridge commencement 1766. 5832: Poem, obituaries, and description of Duke's funeral from newspapers 1768 (ff. 83v, 113v, 114v); description (f. 114) of gold medals for scholastic excellence at Cambridge funded by Newcastle; account (ff. 231v-232) of Duke's installation 1749 as Chancellor of Cambridge. 5852: Newcastle's election and installation 1749 as described (ff. 192-193) by supporter of Prince of Wales.

4. 6832: Newcastle letters (ff. 1-58) to Sir Andrew Mitchell 1748 and 1756-1767. 6834: Lord Barrington's description (f. 37) of Newcastle's last audience 1762 with George III. 6836: copy (f. 60) of Newcastle to Count Bentinck 1756.

5. 6911: Copy (f. 14) of Edward Aller, consul at Naples, to Newcastle 1742 about arrival of British squadron and Duke to Lord Bath (f. 17) about same.

6. 9202-9232: Notes, abstracts, and draft manuscript for Coxe's *Pelham Administration* (320).

7. 9828: Newcastle to Sir John Eardley Wilmot (f. 105) 1766.

8. 11385-11387: Newcastle correspondence with Lord Hyndford, ambassador to Russia, 1748-1749. 11385, p. 547, Pelham to Hyndford 1748 about expense of Russian treaty. Listed but not indexed in *List of Additions to the Manuscripts in the British Museum in the Years 1836-1840* (London: Museum Trustees, 1843), pp. 7-8.

9. Egerton 929: Letter 1747 to Newcastle from Rear Admiral Sir Peter Warren concerning troops for Nova Scotia. *Catalogue of Additions to the Manuscripts in the British Museum in the Years 1841-1845* (London: Museum Trustees, 1850), 1841 section, p. 71.

The following papers are calendared and indexed (pp. 62 and 96) in *Catalogue of Additions to the Manuscripts in the British Museum in the Years 1846-1847* (London: Museum Trustees, 1864, reprinted 1964).

10. 15855: copies (ff. 44, 47, 64, 154) of Admiral George Anson to Newcastle 1740 and 1742 (p. 48). 15956: Newcastle letter (f. 292) 1762 to Thomas Anson (p. 142).

11. 15866-15875: Newcastle correspondence 1735-1755 with James and Solomon Dayrolle, English residents at the Hague and Brussels, and others (pp. 60-78). Pelham letters to S. Dayrolle, 15869, f. 173 (1747); 15870, f. 229 (1748); 15872, ff. 59, 63 (1750).

The following papers are calendared in *Catalogue of the Additions to the Manuscripts in the British Museum in the Years 1854-1875* (London: Museum Trustees, v.1, 1875, v.2, 1877). The *Index* was published separately in 1880 (see pp. 1124-1125).

12. 20799, f. 114, Newcastle's answer 1745 to memorial on wine duties (v.1, p. 268).

13. 20847, f. 337, Newcastle letter 1739 to Comte d'Oeyras (v.1, p. 279).

14. 21506, ff. 144-145; Egerton 1733, f. 127, Newcastle to James Dayrolle 1748 and 1751 (v.1, p. 399, and v.2, p. 866).

15. Egerton 1714, ff. 201-202, Newcastle corrrespondence with Countess Dowager of Portland 1750 (v.2, p. 863).

16. 21551, f. 56, Pelham to George Stepney, undated (v.1, p. 464).

17. 22536: Newcastle letters (ff. 57, 131, 151) among copies of official despatches from John, Lord Carteret, to Newcastle 1743 (v.1, p. 660).

18. 22628, f. 66, Newcastle to Countess of Suffolk 1761; f. 80, Pelham to George Berkeley 1717 (v.1, p. 701).

19. 23627-23629, Newcastle's instructions 1730-1741 to James O'Hara, 2nd Baron Tyrawly, ambassador to Portugal, and Admiral Sir John Norris; 23630, f.49, Newcastle to Tyrawly 1743 (v.1, pp. 870-872, and *Index*, p. 1125).

20. 23780-23830: Pelham and Newcastle letters 1730-1749 to Sir Thomas Robinson, ambassador to Austria; 23812, f. 417, 23813, f. 237, and 23816, ff. 100 and 156, Newcastle letters 1742-1744 to Admiral Thomas Mathews; 23827, f. 272, Newcastle to Count Bentinck 1748 (v.1, pp. 908-909, and *Index*, pp. 1124-1125).

21. Egerton 1721, f. 282, 1722, 6 letters, 1733, f. 120, and 1862, f. 92, Newcastle to Count Bentinck 1748-1753 and 1760-1761 (v.2, pp. 864, 866, and 898, and *Index*, p. 1125).

22. 25560-25561: Petitions to Newcastle from the South Seas Company 1721-1747 (v.2, p. 202).

23. 27732-27735: Pelham and Newcastle correspondence 1732-1736 with Lord Essex, ambassador to Turin (v.2, pp. 350-351, and *Index*, p. 1124).

24. 28051: Newcastle private letters (ff. 351-357) to his brother-in-law 4th Duke of Leeds 1748-1753 (v.2, p. 404).

25. 28103: Newcastle letters (ff. 111-113) to 3rd Earl of Albemarle 1767 (v.2, p. 425).

26. 29589B: Newcastle letter (f. 14) to Lady Isabella Finch c. 1745 (v.2, p. 677).

The following papers are calendared and indexed (p. 539) in *Catalogue of the Additions to the Manuscripts in the British Museum in the Years 1876-1881* (London: Museum Trustees, 1882).

27. 30867: Copy (f. 197) of Newcastle letter 1762 to Charles Wyndham, 2nd Earl of Egremont. 30877: Newcastle letter (f. 13) 1759 to John Wilkes (p. 124).

28. Egerton 2528-2529: Newcastle letters 1739-1742 to Admiral Nicholas Haddock (p. 308).

The following papers are calendared and indexed (p. 791) in *Catalogue of Additions to the Manuscripts in the British Museum in the Years 1888-1893* (London: Museum Trustees, 1894).

29. 33356: Newcastle's copy of statutes of University of Cambridge to 1741 (p. 3).

30. 33441: Pelham letters (ff. 4-6) to Newcastle 1740 (p. 21).

31. 33442: Accounts of repairs to Newcastle's residences 1714-1720 (p. 21).

32. 33627-33628: Personal accounts of Duchess of Newcastle 1737-1776 (p. 89).

33. 34523: Copies (ff. 85-179) of Newcastle correspondence 1754-1768 with Lord Mansfield and others (p. 348).

34. 34524-34525: Copies of Newcastle letters to Hardwicke 1734-1760 (p. 348).

35. Add. Charter 36450-36451: Conveyance by Newcastle of honour and castle of Hastings 1715 (p. 359).

36. Egerton 2687-2691: Newcastle correspondence 1740-1743 with Walter Titley, envoy to Denmark (pp. 452-453).

37. 34728: Newcastle's letters (c.20) 1761-1768 to James West, M.P. 34736: Treasury papers include provisions for West Indies squadron 1741 (ff. 3-22), Civil List and pensions 1742-1745 (ff. 1 and 27-32), and West's notes (f. 109) on cider tax debate 12 March 1763 with vote totals on five questions and list of peers with their votes. *Catalogue...1894-1899*, pp. 60 and 1214.

38. 36586: Account book 1764-1770 for Newcastle's Sussex estates. 36587: Account book of Pelham's estates after 1767 division. *Catalogue of Additions to the Manuscripts in the British Museum in the Years 1900-1905* (London: Museum Trustees, 1907), pp. 145-146 and 775.

39. 37394-37397: Copies of Newcastle correspondence 1724-1725 with diplomats Charles Whitworth, Alexander Hume-Campbell (Lord Polwarth), and Horatio Walpole. *Catalogue of Additions to the Manuscripts in the British Museum in the Years 1906-1910* (London: Museum Trustees, 1912), pp. 27 and 650.

40. 38161: Hardwicke's notes on speeches and debates in Parliament 1717-1763. 38191: Newcastle letter (f. 139) 1762 to Charles Jenkinson. 38197: Letter (f. 39) to Pelham 1746 from Lt. Gen. Thomas Wentworth and copies (ff. 187-189) of Newcastle letters 1761 to John Stuart, 3rd

Earl of Bute. *Catalogue of the Additions to the Manuscripts in the British Museum in the Years 1911-1915* (London: Museum Trustees, 1925), pp. 78, 93, 95, and 1187-1188.

The following papers are calendared and indexed (p. 1110) in *Catalogue of the Additions to the Manuscripts in the British Museum 1921-1925* (London: Museum Trustees, 1950).

41. 40765: Letters (ff. 7-9) to Newcastle 1755 from Thomas Hay, Lord Dupplin (p. 175)

42. 40815-40817: Copies of Newcastle correspondence 1739-1742 with Vice Admiral Edward Vernon; also 40827, ff. 1b-21, and 40828, ff. 65-68b (pp. 185-186).

The following papers are calendared and indexed (p. 531) in *Catalogue of Additions to the Manuscripts 1926-1930* (London: Museum Trustees, 1959).

43. 41354: Pelham correspondence (ff. 14-15b) 1753 and Newcastle correspondence (ff. 20-40) 1757-1761 with Samuel Martin Jr., Secretary to the Treasury; also 41356, ff. 11-13b (pp. 24-26).

44. 41504: Copies (ff. 5-233b) of letters to Newcastle 1724-1733 from Brinley Skinner, consul at Leghorn (p. 61).

45. 43412-43433: Newcastle correspondence 1730-1754 with Sir Benjamin Keene, ambassador to Spain. *Catalogue of Additions to the Manuscripts 1931-1935* (London: Museum Trustees, 1967), pp. 141-142 and 728.

46. Newcastle correspondence with John Carmichael, 3rd Earl of Hyndford, 1749-1750 as ambassador to Russia and 1752 as special envoy to Vienna; 45117, ff. 5-20; 45118, ff. 1-98; 45119, ff. 7-105; 45120, *passim*; 45121, ff. 1-125. *Catalogue of Additions to the Manuscripts 1936-1945* (London: Museum Trustees, 1970), pp. 91-92 and 780.

The following papers are calendared and indexed (pp. 1192-1194) in *Catalogue of Additions to the Manuscripts 1946-1950* (London: British Library, 1979).

47. 47012: Copy (f. 112) of Newcastle memorandum 1766 to George III. 47012A: Newcastle letter (f. 27) c. 1743 to John Percival, 2nd Earl of Egmont. 47014A: Pelham correspondence (ff. 12-14, 18) 1743 with Egmont (p. 215). 47096, ff. 146-22, reversed: Egmont's essay, c. 1746, on Pelham's administration (p. 226).

48. Egerton 3413 and 3437: Pelham correspondence 1749-1752 with Robert Darcy, 4th Earl of Holdernesse, minister to United Provinces and Secretary of State (pp. 316 and 320). 3403-3412, 3427-3430, 3438,

3441, 3462-3463: Newcastle correspondence 1744-1761 with Holdernesse (pp. 315-323). Collection includes many copies of Newcastle letters to others.

49. Newcastle correspondence 1727 with Horatio Walpole, ambassador to France; 48981, ff. 198, 208, 222, 237, 243; 48982, f. 77. *Catalogue of Additions to the Manuscripts 1951-1955* (London: British Library, 1982), pp. 238 and 581.

As of 1996, no catalogue or index had been published for the next three collections, although a provisional catalogue of the Holland House Papers is held in the Manuscripts Room. All three collections contain much material about the Pelham brothers.

50. 51379: Pelham letters (ff. 52-98b) 1743-1751 and Newcastle letters (ff. 1-41b) 1748-1761 to Henry Fox, 1st Baron Holland. 51380: Correspondence (ff. 58-72) of James Waldegrave, 2nd Earl Waldegrave, with Newcastle and Andrew Stone 1752-1761.

51. 57834: Minutes of Cabinet meetings 1748-1765. The Grenville Papers (57804-57837) are available on microfilm from the Center for Research Libraries, Chicago, and in the Manuscripts Room as Microfilm 959.

52. 58283: Newcastle correspondence 1747-1760 with diplomat Sir Andrew Mitchell. Collection is 58283-58367.

53. 61353: Letters (7) 1715-1717 concerning Newcastle's marriage. 61441: Newcastle correspondence 1717-1739 with Sarah, Duchess of Marlborough. Newcastle letters (61496, f. 151, and 61603, f. 215) 1718-1722 to Charles Spencer, 3rd Earl of Sunderland. Letters to Newcastle 1719: 61496, f. 22; 61605, ff. 185-186; 61686, f. 52. 61603: Newcastle memorial (f. 170) 1720 to Treasury Commissioners. 61668: Pelham letters (ff. 159-162b) ?1728 to Sunderland. 61684: Copy (f. 153) of Newcastle letter 1730 to John, 3rd Baron Trevor. *Catalogue of Additions to the Manuscripts, The Blenheim Papers* (London: British Library, 1985), pp. 54, 74, 98-99, 118-119, 136, 146-147, and 707.

54. 61860: Copies (ff. 125-126) of letters to Newcastle from Prince Ferdinand of Brunswick and draft letter 1761 about Ferdinand (ff. 121-124v) from Treasury Board to Marquess of Granby. *British Library Catalogue of Additions to the Manuscripts 1976-1980* (London: British Library, 1995), p. 575.

55. 63093: Copy (f. 71) of Newcastle letter to John Murray, 2nd Earl of Dunmore 1743. *British Library Catalogue of Additions to the Manuscripts 1981-1985* (London: British Library, 1994).

56.   63749A, f. 46, and 63750, ff. 42-45v, Newcastle drafts and copies to Horatio Walpole 1724 and 1755; 63750, f. 26, Newcastle note to ?Lord Harrington 1730.

57.   64813: Newcastle letters (ff. 1-3v) to Duchess 1738-1742 and letters (ff. 4-18) to the Duke and his agents 1757-1768.

58.   69093: In art. 2, Newcastle correspondence with Lady Yarmouth and Lord Henley 1760 and copy of Newcastle's notes of two conversations between Pitt and Prussian ambassador 1760.

59.   70990: Newcastle letter (f. 55) to Sir Thomas Robinson 1755.

60.   Deposit 9389: Barrington Papers, not yet BL numbered or catalogued in 1996. Temporary numbering HA 174:1026/6b/63, Newcastle to Lord Barrington 11 May 1767; 1026/13, "Account of the State of the Commissariat 1757-1761", and /13c, copy letter from Treasury Board about this report, with other letters, 19 May 1761; 1027/112/35-46, Newcastle letters to Barrington 1758-1767. This collection includes many papers relating to the Admiralty, War Office, and Treasury.

61.   King's Manuscripts 55-59: Copies of Newcastle naval correspondence 1726-1728. See 33028 for copies of letters to Vice Admiral Francis Hosier (55-56) notated by Newcastle. *Catalogue of Royal and King's Manuscripts in the British Library* (London: Museum Trustees, 1921), p. 14.

62.   Stowe 247: Newcastle letter (f. 164) to James Craggs Jr. 1720 about Nottingham politics. Stowe 263: Copy (ff. 15v-18v) of Newcastle's paper 18 February 1760 about Belle Isle project, relations with Frederick II of Prussia, and domestic politics. *Catalogue of the Stowe Manuscripts in the British Museum* (London: Museum Trustees, 1896, 2 vols.), v.1, pp. 328 and 342.

63.   Sloane Manuscripts: Newcastle letters to Sir Hans Sloane (4076, ff. 150-158b, 160, 163-165, and 4077, f. 286) 1719-1729. *Index to the Sloane Manuscripts in the British Museum* (London: Museum Trustees, 1904).

Nottingham University Library Manuscripts Department, Hallward Library, University Park, Nottingham NG7 2RD.

64.   Arundell Papers (Ga 12777): Pelham letters (22) to his brother-in-law Richard Arundell 1740-1742 and Newcastle letters (4) to Arundell 1750-1756 on family and personal matters and national and international affairs.

65.   Portland Papers (PwF 7435-7605): Newcastle letters (97) to 3rd Duke of Portland 1763-1768 together with copies and extracts of Newcastle letters to and from others and drafts of Portland to Newcastle.

66.   Newcastle (Clumber) Papers: Pelham's secretary John Roberts kept a portion of Pelham's papers after his death, which apparently are lost. The portion inherited by Pelham's daughter was incorporated into this collection, the papers of Pelham's son-in-law and nephew Henry Clinton, 9th Earl of Lincoln and 2nd Duke of Newcastle, and his descendants. The papers are grouped roughly by topic and date in unbound batches. Letters are numbered individually but are not catalogued individually. NRA has a copy of the catalogue (NRA 7411 Pelham). No index exists for this collection.

a. NeC 36-78: Copies and extracts of official correspondence 1725-1732, chiefly to and from Newcastle, about West Indies and Dunkirk. NeC 79-93: Letters from Horatio Walpole 1725-1746. NeC 94-101: Letters to Pelham from Lord Essex and Newcastle and to the Duke from Walpole, Hardwicke, and Benjamin Keene 1732-1738. NeC 108-128: Letters 1740-1748 include copies of Pelham to Thomas Orby Hunter 1746, Princess of Orange 1747, and Lord Middlesex (2) 1747 and letters to Pelham or Newcastle from Lord Tyrawly 1740, William Pulteney (2) 1740-1741, Hardwicke 1744, Lord Hartford 1745, and Andrew Stone 1746.

b. NeC 129-177: Letters to Pelham from Stone (4) 1740 and 1748, Walpole 1740, Lord Orford (8) 1742-1743, Newcastle 1741; Pelham drafts to Newcastle (8) 1741 and 1748 and Cumberland 1747; to Pelham, all 1748, from Cumberland (2), Sandwich, Sir Thomas Robinson, Bedford, Hardwicke, Hunter; from Newcastle (4) 1748 and 1750, plus many copies of others' letters sent to the Duke. NeC 178-194: Letters to Pelham from Sir Robert Munro 1741, Robinson (2) 1744, Velters Cornwall 1745, Sir Charles Hanbury Williams 1745, Lady Yarmouth 1746, Richmond 1746, James West n.d., Lord Gower (2) 1746-1747. NeC 195-213: Financial papers relating to foreign rulers and states and remitting money for troops abroad; letters about these topics from J. Scrope 1743, J. Gore 1744, J. FitzGerald 1744.

c. NeC 214: Pensions list 1742. NeC 215-225: Military correspondence includes copy of Council minutes 1742 and letters to Pelham from Lord Ligonier 1745-1746, General J. Wentworth (5) 1747, Lord Albemarle 1747, General John Huske 1747. NeC 226-235: Copies of Newcastle-Carteret correspondence 1743. NeC 236-274: Letters to Pelham from Dr. Mich. Lee Dicker 1743-1749. NeC 275-278: Papers about George Anson's resignation of his flag 1744. NeC 279-288: Lord Tyrawly letters from Russia 1744-1745. NeC 289-298: Pelham correspondence with Earl of Westmorland 1744-1753. NeC 299-300: "Lord Chancellor's Paper as settled with D of N, D of D, Lord H and Mr P."

d. NeC 301-336: Letters and papers concerning mainly taxation. NeC 337-352: Papers and letters concerning mainly subsidies to foreign states. NeC 353-367: Letters to Pelham from Lord Chesterfield 1745-1753. NeC 369-378: Letters to Pelham from Lord Morton in France 1744-1746. NeC 379-385: Miscellaneous papers 1745-1746. NeC 386-394: Letters (3) from Lord Harrington at Hanover 1745 and one Pelham reply; from Lord Dunmore (5) 1745-1746 on Rebellion. NeC 395-418: Letters (19) from Sir Everard Fawkener to Pelham 1745-1748 and one Pelham reply 1745, plus related material. NeC 419-446: Papers and letters relating to Spain 1746-1754 include letters from Keene (21) and Walpole. NeC 447-453: William Pitt to Pelham 1746-1754. NeC 454-460: Letters from foreign diplomats at Bonn 1746-1747. NeC 461-472: Correspondence about 1747 election and peace negotiations 1746-1747; letters to Pelham from Sandwich (9) and Cumberland (2). NeC 473-479: Peace proposals and the like 1747.

e. NeC 480-484: Hanaper Office papers. NeC 485-502: Horatio Walpole letters to Pelham 1747-1754. The following 1748 bundles also include many copies Newcastle sent Pelham of his correspondence with others. NeC 555-570: Letters on foreign affairs to Pelham early 1748 from Sandwich, H. B. Legge, Stone, Sir John Mordaunt and Pelham drafts to Cumberland and Lord Mayor of London. NeC 571-588: May 1748 letters from Legge, William Cayley, Newcastle, Cumberland, Fox, and Pelham drafts (3) to Cumberland. NeC 589-620: June 1748 letters from Stone, Legge, Newcastle, Cumberland, Keene, Williams, Hyndford, and Pelham draft to Cumberland. NeC 621-671: July 1748 letters from Sandwich with two Pelham replies, Newcastle (10), Bedford, Cumberland, Cayley, Legge, Stone, Hardwicke, Mordaunt, and Pelham drafts (5) to Newcastle. NeC 672-740: August 1748 letters from Sandwich, Robinson, Newcastle (8) with three Pelham replies, Bedford, Legge, Stone with Pelham reply, Hardwicke, Ossorio with Pelham reply.

f. NeC 741-772: September 1748 letters from Sandwich, Robinson, Newcastle (10) with three Pelham replies and two Pelham to Cumberland, Legge, Stone, Hardwicke, Albemarle, Sir John Barnard, Richard Leveson-Gower, Edward Wortley Montagu, Ossorio. NeC 773-814: October 1748 letters from Sandwich, Robinson with reply, Newcastle (8) with six Pelham replies, Cumberland with reply, Legge, Hardwicke, Hunter, Barnard. NeC 815-836: November-December 1748 letters from Sandwich, Robinson, Newcastle (8) with two replies, Cumberland with reply, Legge, Henry Campion, reply to Stone, and Hardwicke. NeC 837-838: Translation of Definitive Treaty 1748. NeC 839-846: Papers about Treaty 1748. NeC 847-852: Papers 1748-1751 about ambassadors' allowances, payments to Russia, secret service money. NeC 853-857: Miscellaneous papers 1748 include letters from George Lyttelton and Dudley Ryder. NeC 858-863: Military papers 1748-1749.

g. NeC 864-871: Letters from Marquis de Tabuerniga 1748-1751 to John Roberts. NeC 872-878: Papers on foreign affairs include letter from Williams. NeC 879-894: Lord Holdernesse letters to Pelham 1749-1750. NeC 895-904: Papers mainly financial 1749-1750 include letters from William Woods, Lord Rochford, J. Pitt. NeC 905-926: Papers on elections and finance, with letters from Princess of Hesse, Lord Irwin, John Norris, Mr Ridley, Lord Cornbury. NeC 927-936: Letters from Count Bentinck, Robert Keith, Mons. Deneken, S. Dayrolles, Elector of Mayance, and reply to Sir Daniel Lambert. NeC 937-966: Newcastle letters to Pelham May-July 1750. NeC 967-980: Pelham letters to Newcastle April-July 1750. The following bundles also include many papers and copies of letters to and from others Newcastle sent to Pelham. NeC 981-1034: Letters from Stone with reply, Williams, Princess of Orange, reply to Keith. NeC 1035-1047: Miscellaneous papers on foreign affairs July-September 1750. NeC 1048-1084: Newcastle letters (13) to Pelham with two replies August-September 1750.

h. NeC 1085-1106: Papers on foreign affairs August-September 1750 with letter from Mirepoix. NeC 1107-1150: Newcastle letters (21) to Pelham with six replies September-October 1750. NeC 1151-1193: Newcastle letters (11) to Pelham with four replies October-December 1750; Pelham to Harrington; Holdernesse, Albemarle, Bentinck, Count von Haslang to Pelham; Pelham to Stone. NeC 1194-1199: Correspondence about Spain September-October 1750 includes Keene letter. NeC 1201-1212: Papers relating to Nova Scotia 1750-1751. NeC 1213-1217: Fox letters to Pelham 1750-1753. NeC 1218-1221: Letters to Pelham from Newcastle (2), Lord Trentham with reply 1751. NeC 1222-1228: Letters 1751-1752 concerning Tabuerniga's debts. NeC 1229-1240: Correspondence about patronage 1751-1753; letters from Col. Trelawny, Lord Hyde, Irwin, Lord Townshend with reply. NeC 1241-1245: Letters from H. Potts and George Shelvocke of the Post Office, Lord Bury, Hardwicke 1751-1754.

i. NeC 1246: Abstract of transactions of H. M. Commissaries at Paris 1752. NeC 1247-1261: Copies of correspondence on foreign affairs March-May 1752. NeC 1262-1302: Newcastle letters (25) to Pelham with 16 replies April-July 1752. NeC 1303-1355: Memoranda and extracts on foreign affairs March-August 1752. NeC 1356-1369: Copies of Newcastle's correspondence June-August 1752 plus Claudius Amyand to Pelham. NeC 1370-1400: Newcastle letters (25) to Pelham with six replies August-November 1752. NeC 1401-1452: Copies of Newcastle correspondence February and August-October 1752; Keith and Albemarle to Pelham. NeC 1453-1462: Copies September 1752. NeC 1463-1469: Copies of correspondence concerning ecclesiastical preferments 1752. NeC 1470-1477: Letters 1752 to Pelham from Albemarle, S. Fluyder (about Kay's flying shuttle), Abraham Hume, R. Edgecombe. NeC 1478-1483: Miscellaneous letters 1752-1753 including John Coade to Pelham. NeC 1484-1489: Newcastle letters (5) to Pelham 1753; Council meeting minutes 25 July.

j. NeC 1490-1502: Letters to Pelham 1753 from Albemarle, Lord Tankerville, Peter Leigh. NeC 1503-1507: Earl of Leicester to Pelham 1754; minutes of meetings [Cabinet?] 18 March and 9 April; drafts of message about separating Hanover from Crown of Great Britain. NeC 1509-1527: Miscellaneous papers 1751-1760 including election papers for Totness and Cornwall. NeC 1528-1532: Letters relating to Pelham's death and custody of his papers [see NeC 14869b, Robert's will, which refers to papers in his possession]; his draft letter on civilizing Highlands; Hardwicke (4) to Roberts. NeC 1533: Schedule of Court Books 1762-1763 for Pelham manors in Sussex.

k. Irish Affairs. NeC 1534-1545: Chesterfield letters to Pelham 1745-1756. NeC 1546-1564: Letters 1746-1750 from George Stone, Bishop of Winchester, Harrington, and others; Pelham draft. NeC 1565-1576: Letters 1752-1753 from Sackville with reply, Stone, Henry Boyle, Ryder. NeC 1577-1592: Letters 1753-1754 from Sackville, Dorset with reply, Stone. NeC 1593-1598: Papers 1734-1753 on Irish finance including letters from West. NeC 1599-1605: Materials relating to Irish pensions 1741-1752. NeC 1606: Book on Irish trade 1744-1751. NeC 1607: Papers about Irish revenue 1754 include letter from Nicholas Hardinge.

l. Scottish Affairs. NeC 1608-1613: Papers relating to Scottish revenue 1742-1743. NeC 1614-1619: Papers about forfeited estates 1744-1747. NeC 1620-1651: Letters to Pelham August-November 1745 from Brig. Gen. William Blakeney, Gen. John Cope, Marquis of Tweeddale, Duke of Argyll, Lord Fortrose, Duke of Montrose; Pelham drafts (3) to Sir H. Hoghton. NeC 1652-1656: Accounts of battles September-October 1745. NeC 1657-1706: Letters to Pelham 1745 from Blakeney, Allan Whitefoord, Lord Mark Kerr, Gen. James Oglethorpe, Gen. J. Wentworth with reply, Cope, Gen. John Huske, Field Marshal George Wade with reply, Tyrawly, Gen. Charles Howard, Brig. J. Mordaunt. NeC 1707-1725: Papers about Army 1745-1746 with letters to Pelham from Blakeney, Wentworth, Huske, Lord Sutherland, George Johnstone, Sir Conyers D'Arcy, Duncan Forbes, Humphrey Bland. NeC 1726-1748: Sir Everard Fawkener letters to Pelham 1745-1748 with two replies. NeC 1749-1764: Cumberland to Pelham 1745-1747 with five replies. NeC 1765-1772: Letters from Huske and Albemarle 1746-1747.

m. Scottish Affairs. NeC 1773: "Supply for 1714". NeC 1774-1790: Papers 1744-1746 concerning disaffected persons, rebels, and the Pretender. NeC 1791-1809: Papers 1744-1753 include Pelham to Earl of Hopetoun and letters from Sir Ludovick Grant, Sir Thomas Brand, William Earl. NeC 1810-1814: Papers 1746-1747 relating to rebels. NeC 1815-1830: Papers 1746-1752 relating to Commissioners of Customs include Pelham to Commissioners and Jos. Tudor and from Lt. Gen. Churchill. NeC 1831-1838: Petitions 1746-1748 for patronage or reparations. NeC 1838-1841: Letters 1746-1747 from David Blair and James Fordyce. NeC 1842-1865: Letters 1746-1748 from Edinburgh Post Office and miscellaneous writings on Scots topics. NeC 1866-1882: Letters 1746-1748 about elections from William Dalrymple, George Drummond, James Erskine, Forbes, Grant, Lord March, Sir Harry Munro. NeC 1883-1891: Letters 1746-1754 about Jacobites and from Sir John Barnard, Erskine, Edward Edlyn. NeC 1892-1902: Memorials and memoranda 1745-1746 about bills relating to Scotland.

n. Scottish Affairs. NeC 1903-1911: Miscellaneous memorials and petitions 1745-1747. NeC 1912-1945: Letters 1747 about Scottish elections from Hume-Campbell, Drummond, George and Lawrence Dundas, Andrew Fletcher, Forbes, Sir Charles Gilmour, Duke of Gordon, Grant, Patrick Haldane, James Kerr, Capt. George Mackay. Capt. John Maxwell, Lord Morton, Lord Reay. NeC 1946-1956: Argyll letters to Pelham 1747. NeC 1957-1960: Papers 1747-1748 about justice, finance, and tobacco trade. NeC 1961-2007: Letters 1747-1752 from William Grant, Argyll, T. Blackwell, Gen. Bland, Hume-Campbell, Drummond, Lord Findlater, Baron Idle, Fletcher, Charles Erskine, Lord Lauderdale, Mackay, Charles Maitland, Jo. Maule, Morton, Earl of Rothes. NeC 2008-2015: Miscellaneous papers 1747-1751. NeC 2016-2018: Letters from Robert Dundas with reply 1747 and Robert Dundas Jr. 1753. NeC 2019-2024: Papers relating to the Highlands 1748-1749. NeC 2025-2031: Claims on Elcho estate 1748. NeC 2032-2035: Petitions for reparations 1750-1752. NeC 2036-2040: Letters from Jos. Tudor 1750, Robert Dundas 1752-1753, Charles Erskine 1752.

o. Scottish Affairs. NeC 2041-2062: Letters and papers 1751-1752 about tobacco trade. NeC 2063-2083: Correspondence and papers 1751-1752 concerning disaffected persons include Pelham drafts to Baron Edlyn, Scottish Customs Commissioners, and Barons of Exchequer. NeC 2084-2085: Memorials and petitions 1751-1753. NeC 2086-2131: Secret intelligence about Jacobites in Britain and France 1751-1755. NeC 2132-2139: Letters 1752 about murder of Colin Campbell. NeC 2140-2150: Papers 1752 relating to revenue and appointments. NeC 2151-2155: Tudor letters to Pelham 1752. NeC 2156-2198: Papers 1752-1753 about disaffected persons. NeC 2199-2202: Letters about Jacobite intelligence 1752-1753. NeC 2203-2209: Papers relating to elections 1753 include Pelham draft to Drummond. NeC 2210-2219: Election papers 1753-1754; Argyll letters (8) to Pelham. NeC 2220-2221: Bland letters to Pelham 1754. NeC 2222: Book of characters of Scots officials. NeC 2224-2225: Memo c. 1752 from Pelham to King about disaffected persons in His Majesty's service in Scotland.

p. Lincoln family correspondence NeC 2491-2597 may contain references to the Pelham brothers. NeC 3022-3081: Newcastle to niece Lady Lincoln 1742-1768. NeC 3082-3134: Newcastle to Lady Lincoln and Pelham to Lincoln 1741-1758. NeC 3152-3211: Newcastle and Duchess letters 1741-1758 to Lincoln; memo on difficulties in forming plan of administration with Pitt; Newcastle to Devonshire. NeC 3238-3340: Newcastle and Duchess to Lincoln 1754-1774. NeC 3556-3634: Newcastle and Duchess to Lincoln 1751-1764; Newcastle to William Ashburnham. NeC 3635-3678: Newcastle letters to Lincoln 1741-1758; Duke's political papers; Newcastle letters to Andrew Stone, Hardwicke, Baron Münchhausen, John Clevland. NeC 3679-3742: Newcastle letters to Lincoln, Halifax, Granby 1762-1765. NeC 3743-3796: Lady Yarmouth letters to Newcastle 1743-1765. NeC 3797-3845: Newcastle and Duchess to Lincoln 1756-1763. NeC 3846-3896: Lady Yarmouth to Newcastle 1750-1767. NeC 3897-3974: Newcastle to Lincoln 1749-1768.

q. NeC 4066-4095: Pelham to Henry Reade 1749-1752. NeC 4174-4215: Papers relating to naval and military engagements 1759-1762. NeC 4263-4295: Papers concerning Newcastle's expenses and estates and Pelham's personal estate. NeC 4296-4311: Newcastle and Pelham letters 1753-1768 to Mansfield; will for Pelham drafted by Mansfield. NeC 4386-4399: Newcastle and Pelham personal and estate papers 1715-1765. NeC 4415-4461: Among personal and estate papers 1747-1790 are "copy of Prince of Wales's paper June 1747", memo on education of Prince of Wales 1752, and memo in King's hand 1750. NeC 14867-15008 includes much correspondence about Coxe's *Pelham Administration*. NeC 15278: George II reply 1730 to Newcastle. NeC 15281: Pelham letter 1736.

NeC 15286-15288: Newcastle to Mr Sharpe and Mr Speaker 1755-1760. NeC 15289-15291: Henry Hoare to Newcastle and Duchess 1755-1756. NeC 15293: Newcastle to Pitt 1758. NeC 15370a-15371j: Newcastle letters 1727, 1728, 1735.

r. NeS 101-136 and 140-142: Surveys and valuations of portions of Newcastle's properties. NeS 137-139: Description and valuation of Pelham's Sussex estate 1756-1757. Some of the accounts in NeA may be pertinent. NeD 92-162: Newcastle and Pelham deeds and estate settlements. NeD 492-505: Mortgages on Sussex property including Esher. NeE 60: Book on Newcastle's collieries in Northumberland. NeE 61-73: Miscellaneous bundle includes Newcastle and Duchess letter to Lincoln 1765. NeL 542-550b and 758-767: Papers from lawsuit over disposition of Pelham's estate includes copy of his will.

Public Record Office, Ruskin Avenue, Kew, Richmond, Surrey TW9 4DU. (E-mail number to be announced on the Public Record Office home page, http://www.open.gov.uk/pro/prohome.htm)

The PRO publishes its *Current Guide* in microfiche sets that are updated yearly. Part I gives the administrative history of each department. Part II lists the documents alphanumerically by their group letters (department code) and numbered classes (subdivisions), together with general information on the types of documents and time period each subdivision covers. Part III is an index. This set does not include the class lists of individual documents. The fiche sets are owned by a number of larger university libraries and might be available for loan. *Guide to the Contents of the Public Record Office* (London: HMSO, 1963-1968, 3 vols.) is out of date but still of some use. *Public Record Office Lists and Indexes* (London: HMSO, 1892-1936, reprinted by Kraus, 1963, 55 vols.) and the *Supplementary Series* (New York: Kraus Reprints, 1969-1977, 16 vols.) are now out of date and have been revised or replaced at the PRO. They are, nevertheless, still useful for a preliminary search because the divisions within a category of documents (Treasury Papers, for instance) and their numbering have, for the most part, been retained. The Kraus reprints were made from the annotated and revised copies at the PRO and hence are more useful than the original printed volumes. *List & Index Society* publications (London: Swift, 1965-, 261+ vols.) and *List & Index Society Special Series* (London: Swift, 1968-, 26+ vols.) cover mainly PRO material, but some do list material in other repositories. The relevant ones are cited where appropriate below. The following volumes from the PRO *Lists and Indexes* series list documents from the Pelhams' time in office: v.1, *Index of Ancient Petitions of the Chancery and the Exchequer* (see section of declared accounts of the Pipe and Audit Offices); v.19, *List of Volumes of State Papers Foreign 1577-1781*; v.28, *List of War Office Records*; v.36, *List of Colonial Office Records*; v.43, *List of Volumes of*

State Papers Relating to Great Britain and Ireland; v.53, *An Alphabetical Guide to Certain War Office and Other Military Records*. From the *Supplementary Series*, v.10, *Supplementary List of State Papers Domestic and Foreign* lists the miscellaneous documents in SP 9, including many eighteenth-century pamphlets, and the archives from British legations in SP 110.

67. PRO 30/8 (Chatham Papers): The PRO has prepared a fully annotated calendar with index of these papers, which also is available at NRA. Most of the Pelham brothers' correspondence with William Pitt 1744-1768 is printed in (178). The following from Newcastle were not printed but are calendared in the catalogue: PRO 30/8/51/39-101 to Pitt and Lady Chatham 1755-1765. Letters to and from Newcastle to others are scattered in PRO 30/8/85, 89, 91, and 92.

68. PRO 30/29 (Leveson-Gower Papers): Pelham letters (/1/11/4, 6, 7, 15, 18, 19, 21, 23-26) and Newcastle letters (/1/11/5, 14, 20, 22) 1742-1751 to John Leveson-Gower, Lord Stafford and 1st Earl Gower; Stafford's draft letters (/1/16/1-2) to Pelham.

69. PRO 30/70 (Hoare (Pitt) Papers): Letter (/A/4) from Anthony Todd of the Post Office to Newcastle 1753 about the need to increase the staff; Newcastle letter (/C/24) to Pitt 23 November 1758 concerning Baron G. A. von Münchhausen; Newcastle letter (/D/1) to Pitt 7 February 1761 proposing meeting.

70. Colonial Office Papers: This group (CO) covers America, the West Indies, East Indies, Canadian provinces, and Gibraltar and is divided by colonies in alphabetical order, with each colony's papers listed chronologically. Newcastle as Southern Secretary had charge of the colonies 1724-1748, and much of the original correspondence is from or to him. See *Calendar of State Papers Colonial Series: America and West Indies* (London: HMSO, 1936-1969), v.36-44; *Journal of the Commissioners for Trade and Plantations* (London: HMSO, 1928-1935), six unnumbered volumes for January 1728/9-December 1763; *Acts of the Privy Council Colonial Series* (London: HMSO, 1910-1912), v.3, 4, and 6.

71. Foreign Office Papers: This group (FO) covers material generated by the Secretaries of State. Newcastle's letters can be found in FO 90, where the countries are listed alphabetically and the documents listed chronologically.

72. Privy Council Office: Both Pelhams were members of the Privy Council and should be mentioned in the registers of minutes, reports, and papers (PC 2/85-109 and PC 4/1).

73. State Papers Domestic: This class covers internal correspondence; many

of the papers can be seen only on microfilm. Center for Research Libraries, Chicago, holds microfilm of SP 35-37, 1714-1782. See *List & Index Society v.224: Records Relating to Ministerial Meetings in the Reign of George I 1714-1727* (London: Swift, 1987), documents drawn from SP 35 and SP 43-45, and *State Papers Domestic George I (SP 35): Typescript Calendar Part I 1714-1719* (v.139, 1977); *Typescript Calendar Part II 1719-1722* (v.144, 1978); *Typescript Calendar Part III 1722-1725* (v.155, 1979); *Typescript Calendar Part IV 1725-1727 and Supplementary Material 1714-1727* (v.165, 1980); *Index to Lists Parts I to IV 1714-1727* (v.173, 1981). SP 36 (George II) is most pertinent to the Pelhams and is partially calendared and indexed in its class list. SP 41 (Military) includes letters (/6) from Pelham as Secretary at War 1724-1730 and letters (/7-21) to Newcastle 1731-1755. SP 42 (Naval) includes letters (/18-36, 58-62) from the Admiralty Board to the Secretaries of State 1724-1754, the Secretaries' correspondence (/77-99, 105-110) with naval commanders 1726-1748, and papers (/141-143) concerning parliamentary inquiries 1739-1742. Almost all material in SP 43 (Regencies) is of interest on the Pelhams. Most pertinent are letters (/5-37) from the Secretaries accompanying the King to Hanover; correspondence (/38-50) relating to Newcastle's visits to Hanover in 1748, 1750, and 1752; and Newcastle's letters (/69-73, 77-94, 100-102, 112-115) to the Secretaries at Hanover. SP 44 (Entry Books) list Newcastle's correspondence about criminals (/80, 82, 84); his out-letters (/123, 128, 130-134); his ecclesiastical and university correspondence (/152-156); his military correspondence (/178, 180-181, 184, 186, 188); his naval correspondence (/221, 223-228); correspondence and minutes of the Lord Justices of the Regency (/292-325).

74.   SP 54 (Scotland) is very fully calendared but not indexed in its class list and contains many Newcastle letters 1724-1754, especially during the Rebellion (/25-39). Irish affairs can be found in SP 63/383-410, letters and papers to and from the Secretaries of State 1725-1748, and SP 67/9-10, Secretaries' out-letter books 1724-1750.

75.   State Papers Foreign comprises the Secretaries' correspondence with British diplomats and ministers of other countries. The countries are arranged roughly alphabetically in SP 71, 75-86, and 88-99. SP 100 contains letters from foreign ministers accredited to the British Court to the Secretaries, arranged by country and date. SP 104 are Secretaries' out-letter books of correspondence with British diplomats arranged by country and date. (Most of Newcastle's are in FO 90, to which it is cross-referenced.) SP 87 (Military Expeditions) includes Newcastle's correspondence with Field Marshal Lord Stair 1743-1748 (/13), with

various generals 1745 (/19), and with the Duke of Cumberland 1747-1748 (/24-25).

76. Treasury Papers: This group is especially important because both Pelham brothers headed the Treasury. Some calendars and indexes of papers in T 1 have been published: William Shaw, *Calendar of Treasury Books and Papers 1742-1745* (London: HMSO, 1903); *List & Index Society Volume 120: Treasury Board Papers (T 1/319-364) Descriptive List and Index 1745-1755* (London: Swift, 1975); *Volume 125: Treasury Board Papers (T 1/365-388)...1756-1758* (1976); *Volume 240: Treasury Board Papers 1759-1764 (T 1/389-436) with Index for /429-436* (1990). Treasury Board letters, reports, and accounts (T 1/313-421) 1744-1762 are listed numerically in the PRO class list and from /319 onward are calendared and indexed. T 4/11-12 are reference books of applications to the Board 1732-1788 and how they were referred. T 11/22-26 are out-letters 1740-1762 concerning customs and excise. T 14/12-14 are out-letters 1733-1769 concerning Ireland (microfilm). T 17/14-18 are out-letters 1743-1764 concerning Scotland. T 22/4-6 are out-letters 1732-1776 on taxes. T 27/26-28 are general out-letters 1741-1764. T 29/29-35 are the Treasury Board Minute Books 1742-1764. Departmental Accounts (T 38) has items scattered throughout which might be of interest. Most obvious are T 38/160-164, Civil List accounts 1741-1759; /200, final disposal of George II's Civil List; /226, sums paid without account 1760-1769; /228-229, pension papers and bounty lists 1756-1782. T 98/3 are supplementary papers, never calendared, of uncertain dates later than 1732.

77. War Office Papers: This group includes a few items from Pelham's service as Secretary at War. WO 4/24-32 are the Secretary's out-letters 1724-1730. WO 8/2 are out-letters concerning Ireland 1721-1731.

Bedford County Record Office, County Hall, Cauldwell Street, Bedford MK42 9AP.

78. Microfiche of Bedford correspondence, part of which is printed in (183). No index exists to these letters. The originals, together with a packet of letters October 1749-May 1750 (including Newcastle's), are held at Woburn Abbey, Woburn MK43 0TP (private: address to Bedford Estates Archivist).

79. Russell Correspondence (R3/113): Newcastle letter to John Russell, 4th Duke of Bedford, 13 July 1762.

Cambridge University Library Department of Manuscripts, West Road, Cambridge CB3 9DR.

80.   Cholmondeley (Houghton) Papers: Pelham letters to Sir Robert Walpole 1725 and 1727 (Ch(H) corres. #1227, 1476, 3306); letters from (22) and to (44) Newcastle 1724-1739; letters to Pelham from Philip Gerss 1725 (#1212), Edward Field 1725 (#1213), J. Selwyn c. 1730 (#1667), and Duke of Rutland 1727 (#1472). NRA catalogue indexes letters.

Chatsworth, Bakewell, Derbyshire DE4 1PP (write to Trustees of the Chatsworth Settlement).

81.   Devonshire Papers (private): Pelham letters 1738-1752 (249/0-70) and Newcastle letters 1725-1764 (182/0-385) to the 3rd Duke of Devonshire and Marquis of Hartington (4th Duke), both William Cavendish. This collection is now arranged chronologically and contains many references to the Pelhams. NRA catalogue indexes each letter. Extracts about Irish affairs from the Pelham brothers' letters can be found in a PRO Northern Ireland volume in the NRA collection (NRA 20594).

Chewton House, Chewton Mendip (Waldegrave estate). Write to Secretary of Historical Manuscripts Commission, Quality House, Quality Court, Chancery Lane, London WC2A 1HP, about access to NRA 28249 Waldegrave.

82.   Waldegrave Papers (private): Collection only roughly catalogued and not indexed. Pelham and Newcastle letters to James Waldegrave, 1st Earl Waldegrave, in box "Letters and despatches 1725-40"; Newcastle letters in boxes "Correspondence with Ambassadors and Duke of Newcastle 1730-40" and "Letters...secret...1734-36" and in bundles labelled 1727-40, 1730, 1732, 1733, 1734, and 1740.

Devon Record Office, Castle Street, Exeter EX4 3PU.

83.   Seymour Papers: Newcastle letters 1730-1737 to Charles Seymour, 6th Duke of Somerset (1392 M/L18/1730/14, /1732/18-19, /1733/25-26, /1737/11); Pelham letters to 6th Duke (1392 M/L18/1730/1, /1740/4, /1743/3-4); Newcastle letters to Edward Seymour, 8th Duke of Somerset (1392 M/L18/1751/9 and /1753/4). Topic primarily politics.

Dorset Record Office, 9 Bridport Road, Dorchester DT1 1RP.

84.   Calcraft Family Papers: D86/x3, Henry Fox's out-letter book as Secretary at War 1746-1754 includes letters to Newcastle; D86/x4, Fox's private out-letters June 1748-May 1754 include letters to Newcastle.

History of Parliament, Wedgwood House, 15 Woburn Square, London WC1H 0NS (Director, Valerie Cromwell).

85.   In the course of compiling the *History of Parliament* volumes, editors have made transcripts of letters in many private collections. Researchers

are sometimes permitted to use these transcripts when a collection is closed. Americans will find a letter of introduction helpful.

House of Lords Record Office, London SW1A 0PW (enquiries to Clerk of the Records).

86. Many of the records, such as committee deliberations, should provide insight into Newcastle's long service in Lords. This Office also holds the few Commons records that survived a fire in 1834. Full information can be found in Maurice Bond, *Guide to the Records of Parliament* (London: HMSO, 1971). The Lostwithiel Election Papers in the House of Commons Library include five Newcastle letters 1754-1763 (Bond, p. 293).

Lambeth Palace Library, London SE1 7JU.

87. MS 1742: Newcastle correspondence (ff. 185-223) 1729 with Bishop of London Edmund Gibson includes Duke's correspondence with Bishop of Lincoln Richard Reynolds. E.G.W. Bill, ed., *A Catalogue of Manuscripts in Lambeth Palace Library* (Oxford: Clarendon Press, 1972), p. 234.

88. MS 2589 (Secker Papers): Copies of papers concerning the American colonies include a paper prepared at Newcastle's request 1745 about appointment of bishops. *Catalogue...Lambeth* (1983).

Lincolnshire Archives Office, The Castle, Lincoln LN1 3AB.

89. Monson Papers 13/1/12-13, account books of Pelham as Paymaster General, kept by his deputy Hon. Charles Monson, M.P., 1730-1747. Whole of section 13 is useful on Pelham in that office, in particular 13/3/13, folder of correspondence 1739-1744 concerning American expedition, and 13/2/XI-XV, correspondence with deputies accompanying military forces. XI is Pelham's correspondence 1740-1742 with George Colebrooke, deputy paymaster for the West Indies expedition, and XV, with Thomas Orby Hunter on the Continent. 25/2/49, William Blakeney to Pelham about troops in Virginia 23 October 1740; 25/2/50, John Colebrook to Pelham from Jamaica 30 March 1742.

Mannington Hall, Norwich NR11 7BB. (Address enquiries to The Lord Walpole.)

90. Horatio Walpole Papers (private): Small bundle of letters (#17/1/38) from Newcastle and others dealing with Anglo-French relations 1754-1756.

National Library of Scotland Department of Manuscripts, George IV Bridge, Edinburgh EH1 1EW

91.   MS 302: Newcastle letters (#5, 7-8, 10, 24, 30, 41) and Pelham letters (#4, 17) August-November 1745 to Field Marshal George Wade; MS 315: Copy (f. 122) of Pelham letter 1752 concerning murder case; MS 578: Pelham letter n.d. (#178); MS 1081: Pelham letter 1745 (f. 10) to ?Robert Dundas. *Catalogue of Manuscripts Acquired Since 1925, Vol. I* (Edinburgh: NLS Trustees, 1938), pp. 46, 47, 80, and 146.

92.   MSS 2967-2970: Newcastle letters (8) 1726-1754 to Duncan Forbes of Culloden. *Catalogue...Vol. II* (1966), pp. 144-146 and 607.

93.   MSS 3733-3736: Newcastle letters (15) 1745-1747 to Major General John Campbell about Jacobite rebellion; Pelham letter MS 3736, #518. *Catalogue...Vol. II* (1966), pp. 284, 607, and 756.

94.   MSS 5073-5078: Newcastle letters (25) 1727-1754 and Pelham letters (5) 1748-1753 to Charles Erskine, Lord Justice Clerk. *Catalogue...Vol. IV* (1982), pp. 13-14, 352, and 470.

95.   MSS 7067, 7073, 7074, 7078: Newcastle correspondence 1745-1752 with 4th Marquess of Tweeddale; MS 7187: Copies (ff. 81, 85v-91, 96, 100-106) of Field Marshal George Wade to Pelham 1726-1728. *Catalogue...Vol. V* (1986), pp. 34, 58-59, 235, and 322.

National Maritime Museum Manuscripts Section, Greenwich, London SE10 9NF.

96.   MS 91/018 (Sandwich Papers): V/19-22, draft despatches from John Montagu, 4th Earl of Sandwich, to Newcastle 1748; V/32, 1746 instructions including Newcastle's private briefing of Sandwich; V/50, Pelham letters (13) 1746-1748; V/51, copies of Sandwich's letters to Pelham 1747-1748; V/53-55, Newcastle letters 1746-1748; V/63-68, despatches from Newcastle and others 1746-1748. Collection contains copies of Newcastle letters to other ambassadors.

97.   VER/1/2 (Vernon Papers): Newcastle correspondence 1740-1742 with Admiral Edward Vernon among papers relating to Porto Bello, Cartegena, and other expeditions in region.

National Register of Archives (Scotland), West Register House, Charlotte Square, Edinburgh EH2 4DF (enquiries about access).

98.   Crichton-Stuart Papers (private): Pelham letter 1727 and Newcastle letter 1725 to Hugh Campbell, 3rd Earl of Loudoun, and drafts (4) to Newcastle (Box 1700-39, Loudoun Papers); Newcastle letter 1747 to

John Campbell, 4th Earl (Box 1740-52). Newcastle letters (c. 60) 1757-1761 to John Stuart, 3rd Earl of Bute (listed individually in NRA catalogue). Refer to NRA(S)0631 when enquiring.

99. Hope-Johnstone Papers (private): Bundle 290, Newcastle correspondence 1765 with John Hope, 2nd Earl of Hopetoun, about proposed appointment of Earl as Lord Privy Seal, which he declined. Refer to NRA(S)0393 when enquiring.

Newport Central Library, John Frost Square, Kingsway, Newport, Gwent NP9 1PA.

100. Sir Charles Hanbury Williams Papers: M411 012, volume of autograph letters 1736-1749 includes at least one from Pelham; qM411 012, letters and papers from Newcastle 1753. No catalogue or index exists for these Papers, which include other diplomatic and private correspondence. See D. B. Horn, "Hanbury Williams MSS.", *Bulletin of the Institute of Historical Research* 2 (1925): 61-62, and his *Sir Charles Hanbury Williams and European Diplomacy* (London: Harrap, 1930), pp. 298-299.

Northamptonshire Record Office, Wootton Hall Park, Northampton NN4 8BQ (enquiries about access).

101. Watson (Rockingham Castle) Papers (private): Press C, #22, 23, 30, and 36, letters between Sir Thomas Pelham and his brother Henry 1703 and 1708 about money matters; #514, summary particulars 1761 of Sussex estates formerly Henry Pelham's, with map, names of tenants, acreages, rents, and types of tenure; #520, particulars, valuations, and map of Sussex estates 1766; #521, Pelham's final account 1722 as Treasurer of the Chamber. Pelham estate papers (#1214-1271) include #1221, project Sept 1737 for paying Newcastle's debts; #1222, 1223, and 1228, Newcastle estate papers; #1225, copy of Pelham's will; #1271, bound volume of maps of Sussex estates 1728-1733.

Oxford University Bodleian Library Department of Western Manuscripts, Broad Street, Oxford OX1 3BG.

102. MSS North: Newcastle letters (d. 6, ff. 23, 24, 98, 129) 1754-1759 and Pelham letter (d.7, f. 201) 1753 to Francis North, 1st Earl of Guilford. See *Summary Catalogue of Post-Medieval Western Manuscripts in the Bodleian Library Oxford, Acquisitions 1916-1975* (Oxford: Clarendon, 1991), 3 vols., for collections in this repository.

103. MSS Autographs: Newcastle letter (b. 4, p. 27B). MSS Donations: Pelham letters (c. 102, ff. 140, 143) to John Tucker, M.P., 1745-1746.

MSS English history: letter (c. 191, f.12) to Newcastle about East India Company; draft letter (c. 314, ff. 41-43b) from George Wade to Pelham 1744.

104. MSS English letters: Newcastle letters (c. 17, ff. 20-21 and 78) to Sir Thomas Pengally c.1720; draft letters to and by Pelham (c. 144, ff. 130-131, 198-201); copies of John Hedges, envoy to Turin, to Pelham (c. 191, pp. 4-5, 13-15) and Newcastle (pp. 52-53) 1726-1727; draft letters (c. 338, ff. 9-10, 21-40) from 4th Earl of Rochford, ambassador to Turin, to Newcastle 1749-1753; Newcastle letters (c. 386, ff. 84-91) to Charles Townshend 1758-1766.

105. MSS Clarendon: Copies (c. 468/1) of Newcastle correspondence 1730-1733 with Benjamin Keene among papers about Anglo-Spanish relations.

Royal Institution of Cornwall, Royal Cornwall Museum, River Street, Truro TR1 2SJ.

106. BRA A.437: Letters to Pelham about parliamentary affairs and elections for various boroughs in Cornwall 1746-1754.

Royal Institute of British Architects, British Architectural Library Manuscripts and Archives Collection, 66 Portland Place, London W1N 4AD.

107. PEL/1: Building accounts ledger 1740-1752 for renovations of and additions to Pelham's home, 22 Arlington Street. Lists wages, artisans and craftsmen, materials, and expenses.

Scottish Record Office, HM General Register House, Edinburgh EH1 3YY.

108. GD157-158: Correspondence of the Earls of Marchmont. Large portion has been printed in *HMC Polwarth* (166) and Rose (189), but many of the printed letters have been sold out of the family. The following were not printed: GD158/2444/1-2, Newcastle letters (7) to Alexander Hume-Campbell (2nd Earl) June 1724-April 1725; /2572, Newcastle to Hugh Hume-Campbell (3rd Earl) 1743.

Sheffield Archives, 52 Shoreham Street, Sheffield S1 4SP.

109. Wentworth Woodhouse Manuscripts: Newcastle correspondence (c.200 items) 1751-1768 with Charles Watson-Wentworth, 2nd Marquis of Rockingham, and others. Pelham letter to Lord Mansfield 1753. Calendared and indexed in *List & Index Society Special Series Volume 19: Wentworth Woodhouse Manuscripts Handlist and Index* (London: Swift, 1984).

West Sussex Record Office, Sherburne House, 3 Orchard Street, Chichester PO19.

110. Goodwood Papers: The Pelhams' correspondence 1732-1750 with Charles Lennox, 2nd Duke of Richmond, is listed and indexed in Francis Steer and J.E.A. Venables, eds., *Catalogue of the Goodwood Estate Archives, Vol. II* (Chichester: West Sussex County Council, 1972). All the letters are printed in McCann (174).

B. CANADA

National Archives of Canada, Ottawa K1A 0N3.

111. MG 18 N34: Newcastle letter 21 September 1758 to Chancellor of the Exchequer Henry Bilson Legge outlining budget prospects and military operations in America, West Indies, and Continent. No copy survives in the Newcastle Papers.

112. MG 21 and 24 A 77: Copies from Newcastle and Hardwicke Papers concerning Canadian naval and military affairs 1747-1762.

C. JAMAICA

Institute of Jamaica, 12-16 East Street, Kingston

113. MSS. Box 3: Letters (68) from Edward Trelawny, Governor of Jamaica, to Pelham 1740-1750 concerning war in West Indies, local affairs, and British politics, especially West Looe, Cornwall. Calendared in K. E. Ingram, *Sources of Jamaican History 1655-1838* (London: Inter Documentation, 1976), v.1, pp. 324 and 326-327.

114. A. 10: Copies of official correspondence between Newcastle and Robert Hunter, Governor of Jamaica, 1727-1733. Calendared in Ingram, v.1, pp. 307-310.

D. UNITED STATES

William L. Clements Library, University of Michigan, Ann Arbor 48109.

See Arlene Shy, *Guide to the Manuscripts Collections of the William L. Clements Library* (Boston: Hall, 1978, 3rd ed.) for the scope of these collections.

115. Sydney Papers: Newcastle's "State of Orders for Reprisals" 1727-1732 concerning Spanish seizures of British ships. Extracts (3) of Newcastle to Sir Benjamin Keene 1735-1737. "The invocation in the beginning...," a parody attacking Newcastle and Walpole. Letters to Pelham from James Ord 1751 on slave trade; Sir Thomas Robinson (2) 1745-1746 on Barbadoes; Sir Dudley Ryder 1750; Thomas Wentworth (2) 1741-1742; Robert Dinwiddie 1744 from Antigua; Corbyn Morris 1748; Benjamin Martyn 1748; James Crokatt 1749; Michael Dicker 1744; George Clinton

1746; Archbishop George Stone (2)1750 from Dublin; 1st Earl of Hardwicke 1750 on Irish monetary problems. Pelham copy to Stone 1750. Outline of proclamation on coinage from Hardwicke. Printed debate 19 December 1745 on sending for Hessian troops.

116. Shelburne Papers: John Johnson to Pelham 1749 on National Debt. Newcastle copy to South Sea Company directors 1737. Abstracts (12) of Sir Benjamin Keene to Newcastle 1729-1732. Copies to Newcastle from Sir Dudley Ryder 1749 and South Sea Company (5) 1735-1737.

117. George Clinton Papers: Clinton drafts to Newcastle (21)1744-1748 and to Pelham 1746. Newcastle letters to Clinton (7) 1744-1747; copies to Board of Trade 1741, William Shirley (2) 1747, and Sir Peter Warren 1745. John Catherwood draft to Pelham 1749.

118. Germain Papers: Newcastle letters to George Sackville Germain 1751, 1755, 1758, 1759; copies to and from Hon. Charles Townshend 1764. Gideon Schaw to Newcastle 1757.

119. Miscellaneous MSS: Jonathan Law to Newcastle 1744. Robert Dinwiddie to Pelham 1743.

120. Lacaita-Shelburne MSS: Newcastle to Sir William Waldegrave 1756.

121. Ligonier Letter Book: Sir John Ligonier copies (5) to Newcastle 1759-1760.

Duke University Special Collections Library, Durham, North Carolina 27708-0185.

122. Walpole Collection: Newcastle letters (2) November 1734 to Sir Robert on Queen's health and foreign affairs.

123. Diplomatic dispatches: Autograph drafts of Newcastle's instructions 1731 to Sir Benjamin Keene in Madrid about disputes with Spain, including Jenkins' ear (2 vols.).

124. Pelham letters to Thomas Osborne, 4th Duke of Leeds, 1748; George Townshend 1749 (2); and copies (2) to William Gordon, 17th Earl of Sutherland, 1747.

125. Harman Verelst Papers: Letters (27) 1741-1745 from agent for Georgia Colony to the Pelhams.

Harvard University Houghton Library, Cambridge, Massachusetts 02138.

126. fMS Eng 803: List of books in Newcastle's library.

127.   Autograph file: Newcastle letters to Company of Rhode Island 1746 and John Sharpe 1747.

128.   bMS Can 2 and 3: Two reports to Pelham concerning Nova Scotia 1725 and 1750.

The Huntington Library Department of Manuscripts, 1151 Oxford Road, San Marino, California 91108.

See *Guide to British Historical Manuscripts in the Huntington Library* (San Marino: Huntington Library, 1982) for the scope of these collections.

129.   Letters (17) to Pelham 1744-1748 from Governor William Shirley of New York.

130.   Hastings Collection 10128-10135: Pelham letters (6) 1724-1729 to James Campbell, 1727 to 3rd Earl of Loudoun, and 1729 to Theophilus Hastings, 9th Earl of Huntingdon; 10136-10139: Newcastle letters (4) 1754 and 1756.

131.   Loudoun Collection 9292-9300 and 12427-12429: Newcastle letters and extracts (12) 1725-1730 and 1742-1746 to 3rd and 4th Earls of Loudoun and others.

132.   Newcastle letters to field commanders (STT 1573) 1745, Sir George Pocock (PO 848) 1762, and 1st Baron Lyttelton (MO 4017) 1764.

Lewis Walpole Library, 154 Main Street, Farmington, Connecticut 06032.

133.   Weston Papers: v.3, Pelham letters (3) to Lord Harrington 1744-1749 on Irish and Scottish affairs; v.4, Pelham letters (2) to Harrington 1749 on Irish revenue; v.5, Newcastle letter, n.d.

134.   Bound manuscript that once belonged to Newcastle: "A Concise Account of the War Begun with Spain in 1739 and with France in 1744. An Account of the Rebellion in Britain in 1745 and 1746".

135.   Sir Charles Hanbury Williams Papers: Diplomatic and private correspondence includes copies of Newcastle official letters and important letters from Henry Fox.

New York Public Library Manuscripts Division, Fifth Avenue and 42nd Street, New York 10018.

136.   Volume of copies of letters between Newcastle, Lt. Gen. James St. Clair, and Admiral Richard Lestock concerning an invasion on the coast of France at Port L'Orient in 1746. Some of the letters are printed in *Bulletin of the New York Public Library* 10 (1906): 303-328.

University of Kansas Kenneth Spencer Research Library, Lawrence, Kansas 66045-2800.

137. MS 101D (Papers of Col. John Armstrong, Chief Engineer): Copies of letters from Armstrong and Horatio Walpole to Newcastle from Paris in 1727 about a conference with Cardinal Fleury (/1a, 21 April NS), their meeting with the Dutch delegates (/2, 21 May NS), and the negotiating position agreed upon with the Dutch (/3, 23 May).

Library of Congress Department of Manuscripts, 101 Independence Avenue SE, Washington, D.C. 20540.

138. Reproductions from the Newcastle and Hardwicke Papers, calendared in Grace Gardner Griffin, *A Guide to Manuscripts Relating to American History in British Depositories* (Washington, D.C.: Library of Congress, 1946), pp. 149-150 and 156-157.

University of California, Bancroft Library Manuscripts Division, Berkeley 94720.

139. Stanhope Papers: 44 bound volumes of correspondence and papers, chiefly diplomatic, 1720-1748 of Philip Dormer Stanhope, 4th Earl of Chesterfield, ambassador to the Hague, Lord Lieutenant of Ireland, and Secretary of State for the Northern Department. V.26: Newcastle letters (#1-41) and Pelham letters (#42-51) 1744-1746; v.28: copies (#169-170) of Chesterfield to Pelham 1745; v.37, Newcastle letters (#628-636) 1745; v.40, Newcastle letters (#779-787) 1746. NRA catalogue describes v.26-42. Bancroft guide (#72/243) covers whole collection. No name index to papers. British Library Department of Manuscripts holds microfilm (M645, 19 reels) of these papers. Newcastle-Chesterfield correspondence 1744-1746, taken from the Newcastle Papers, is printed in Lodge (180).

Yale University Sterling Library Department of Manuscripts and Archives, 130 Wall Street, Box 208240, New Haven, Connecticut 06520-8240.

140. Burnet Family Papers (MS 114, Folder 3): Newcastle letters (7) to Richard West, Lord Chancellor of Ireland, August 1725-April 1726.

141. Film Misc 845: Microfilm (six reels) of folios from Newcastle Papers 33028-33030 and 33046-33049. Film Misc 976: Microfilm (287 reels) of folios from the Newcastle Papers 32686-33078.

Yale University Beinecke Library Osborn Collection, New Haven, Connecticut 06520

142. Osborn Files, Pelham: Letters from Pelham to ?3rd Duke of Argyll

1753, Thomas Orby Hunter 1747, ?Duke of Leeds 1748, Sir Robert Wilmot 1745, and Earl Nugent (5) 1745-1751. Letters to Pelham from Hunter (49) 1743-1748; Robert Trevor, 1st Viscount Hampden (11) 1744-1745; Jasper Clayton 1743; Sir Philip Honeywood 1743; 2nd Duke of Montagu 1742; Sir John Mordaunt (3) 1748; John Nicoll (2) 1748.

143. Osborn Files, Newcastle: Letters from Newcastle to Charles Townshend 1722; Solomon Dayrolles 1725; ?Sir John Goodricke 1732; Charles Townshend 1747; Earl Nugent 1754; Sir Robert Wilmot 1762; 4th Viscount Townshend 1767.

144. Townshend Box 1: /5, anonymous MS 10 July 1714, memorandum concerning Newcastle's marriage settlement; /8, copy of Hon. Charles Townshend to Newcastle 30 April 1764.

145. MS fc.69: Copies (3 vols.) of correspondence October 1740-March 1744 between British secretaries of State (including Newcastle) and their envoys in European capitals concerning primarily hostilities between Austria and Prussia.

2

Published Compilations of Original Papers Containing Pelham Brothers' Letters

A. HISTORICAL MANUSCRIPTS COMMISSION REPORTS

These volumes are surveys of primarily private collections of papers and vary in quality of editing and content. Since few of the letters are given in full, they must be compared with the originals. The long and sometimes confusing titles of the volumes often are cited in short form and by series number. An old but still useful explanation can be found in R. A. Roberts, *The Reports of the Historical MSS. Commission* (New York: Macmillan, 1920). *Guide to the Reports of the Royal Commission on Historical Manuscripts 1870-1911. Part II: Index of Persons* (London: HMSO, 1935 and 1938, 3 vols.) and *Guide...1911-1957. Part II: Index of Persons* (London: HMSO, 1966, 3 vols.) give information on the contents of the numbered volumes, the period each covers, and the short titles commonly used and also index references to persons by volume. Page numbers must be sought in the indexes of the volumes themselves. Although the Pelhams are mentioned in many of the 81 reports, only those printing letters are listed here.

146. *Second Report*. Liechtenstein: Kraus Reprints, 1979.

Pelham letters (3) 1721 and 1728 and Newcastle letters (2) 1721 to Jacob Tonson.

147. *Third Report*. Liechtenstein: Kraus Reprints, 1979.

Newcastle letter to the Earl of Oxford 1717; Newcastle letters 1746-1763 and Pelham letters 1748-1752 to Henry Dundas, Lord Melville.

148. *Fourth Report*. Liechtenstein: Kraus Reprints, 1979.

Newcastle letters (5) to the Duke of Dorset 1753-1754.

149. *Seventh Report.* Liechtenstein: Kraus Reprints, 1979.

Newcastle to Thomas Pengally about Sir Richard Steele c. 1718.

150. *Eighth Report.* Liechtenstein: Kraus Reprints, 1979.

Newcastle letter 1763 in the Braybrooke Papers.

151. *Ninth Report, Part III.* London: Eyre and Spottiswoode, 1884.

Newcastle letters 1751 (3), 1758, 1759 to George Sackville; Pelham letters to Sackville 1751 (2) and 1752 (2); Newcastle to the Duke of Dorset 1752 (2) and 1753; Pelham to Dorset 1754.

152. *Report on the Manuscripts of Mrs. Stopford-Sackville.* London: HMSO, 1904.

Revised and enlarged edition of (151).

153. *Tenth Report, Appendix I.* London: Eyre and Spottiswoode, 1885.

Pelham letters to Lord Harrington 1749 (2); Newcastle to Edward Weston 1762; minutes of Cabinet meeting 29 March 1762.

154. *Calendar of Proceedings of the House of Lords, Vol. X.* London: HMSO, 1911.

Petition 1713 of the Dowager Duchess of Newcastle contesting her husband's will and Pelham and Newcastle answers through a lawyer.

155. *Eleventh Report, Appendix IV.* London: HMSO, 1887.

Newcastle letters to Lord Townshend 1748 and 1754.

156. *Eleventh Report, Appendix V; Fourteenth Report, Appendix X; Fifteenth Report, Appendix I* (Dartmouth Papers I, II, III). London: HMSO, 1887-1896.

I: Newcastle letters 1745 and 1765. II: Newcastle to 2nd Earl of Dartmouth 1765 and 1766. III: Newcastle to Dartmouth 1765.

157. *Twelfth Report, Appendix III* (Cowper Papers III). London: HMSO, 1889.

Newcastle letter 1717 to Vice Chancellor Thomas Coke.

158. *Thirteenth Report, Appendix II* (Portland Papers II). London: HMSO, 1891.

Useful references to the Pelham family in letters of John Holles, Duke of Newcastle, his widow, and Robert Harley, 1st Earl of Oxford, and also in parts

III-VII. (These Harley Papers are available on microfilm (M2003/1-5) in the British Library Manuscripts Room.)

159. *Twelfth Report, Appendix V* (Rutland Papers II). London: HMSO, 1891.

Newcastle letters and extracts (22) 1759-1762 to John Manners, 3rd Marquess of Granby.

160. *Thirteenth Report, Appendix VI*. London: HMSO, 1892.

Pelham letter to John, Lord Carteret, in 1729.

161. *Thirteenth Report, Appendix VII*. London: HMSO, 1893.

Newcastle letter 1733 to the Earl of Lonsdale; Newcastle's minute of Pelham's meeting with George II on 8 April 1745; Newcastle to Sir Robert Wilmot 1762.

162. *Fourteenth Report, Appendix IX*. London: HMSO, 1895.

Pelham letters (15) to Robert Trevor 1741-1746; Newcastle to Trevor 1743 and 1744; Pelham to Francis Hare 1722.

163. *Fifteenth Report, Appendix VI*. London: HMSO, 1897.

Newcastle letters (6) to Charles Howard, 3rd Earl of Carlisle, 1725-1727, 1730, 1756; Pelham to Carlisle 1725.

164. *Report on Manuscripts in Various Collections, Vol. VIII*. London: HMSO. 1901.

Newcastle letters (13) to Viscount Irwin 1745-1750; Pelham to Irwin 1744 and 1745 (2).

165. *Report on the Manuscripts of the Lady Du Cane*. London: HMSO, 1905.

Newcastle letters (5) to Vice Admiral Sir William Rowley and others 1744-1746.

166. *Report on the Manuscripts of Lord Polwarth*. London: HMSO, 1911-1961.

IV: Newcastle letters (39) to Alexander Hume-Campbell, Lord Polwarth, and Charles Whitworth 1724-1725. V: Newcastle letters 1747-1761 to Hugh Hume-Campbell, 3rd Earl of Marchmont, and 1750-1755 to Alexander Hume-Campbell; Pelham letters 1747-1750 to Hume-Campbell.

167. *Report on the Manuscripts of the Earl of Denbigh, Part V*. London: HMSO, 1911.

Newcastle letters to the Earl of Denbigh 1759 and 1760.

168. *Report on the Manuscripts of the late Reginald Rawdon Hastings, Vol. III.* London: HMSO, 1934.

Newcastle letter 1756 to the Earl of Huntingdon.

B. OTHER COLLECTIONS

169. Coxe, William. *Memoirs of the Administration of the Right Honourable Henry Pelham.* London: Longman, 1829. 2 vols.

Prints whole or portions of many letters to and from both Pelham and Newcastle. However, Coxe was blind by this time and relied on assistants to transcribe the letters, which should be checked against the originals for errors. V.1 ends at 1748. The index (v.2) lists the topic for every page reference. This work was reprinted by AMS Press in 1971.

170. Lawson-Tancred, Sir Thomas. *Records of a Yorkshire Manor.* London: Arnold, 1937.

Newcastle inherited property and electoral interest at Aldborough and Boroughbridge. This work describes his activities beginning with the 1713 election and prints Pelham letters from 1734, 1735, and 1746 and 34 Newcastle letters 1713-1767.

171. *The Correspondence of Richard Steele.* Rae Blanchard, ed. Oxford: Clarendon Press, 1941, reprinted 1968.

Prints Newcastle's letter to Steele in December 1719 forbidding most of the Drury Lane staff to appear on stage. Also included are Steele's protesting letters to Pelham and the Duke and an editorial note giving the background of the affair.

172. Yorke, Philip C. *The Life and Correspondence of Philip Yorke Earl of Hardwicke.* Cambridge: Cambridge University Press, 1913. 3 vols.

This biography of Newcastle's closest friend is well edited, with extensive annotation. A narrative of events precede each section of illustrative letters, most of which are edited and must be compared with the originals. Many letters between Newcastle and Hardwicke are included, with fewer of Pelham's. Letters from others, especially the Yorkes, illuminate the period. Notation indicates whether copies of Newcastle's letters can be found in both his Papers (1) and Hardwicke's (2) or only latter. V.1 covers period to 1748 and includes character studies of both Pelhams (pp. 284-88), very perceptive on Newcastle; v.2, 1748-60; v.3, 1760-64. An extensive and thorough index (v.3) lists entries for persons by topics of references.

173. Harris, George. *The Life of Lord Chancellor Hardwicke.* London: Moxon, 1847. 3 vols.

Prints many quotations from Newcastle's letters in the Hardwicke Papers and also letters between the Yorkes which contain information about the Duke. Index (v.3) lists all references to Newcastle. Not as extensive or reliable as Yorke (172).

174. *The Correspondence of the Dukes of Richmond and Newcastle 1724-1750.* Timothy J. McCann, ed. Lewes: Sussex Record Society, 1984.

Includes both brothers' letters to Richmond, their good friend and political ally in Sussex. Archival reference numbers for Newcastle and Goodwood (110) Papers are listed with each letter. The annotation supplies complete identification of persons and events mentioned, making this edition an invaluable source on national and county politics.

175. *The Letters of Thomas Burnet to George Duckett 1712-1722.* David Nichol Smith, ed. Oxford: Roxburghe Club, 1914.

Prints (p. 189) Newcastle's letter May 1727 to Thomas Burnet, British Consul at Lisbon, about Burnet's quarrel with the British ambassador. Taken from the Burnet Papers, Bodleian MS Add. d. 23, f. 140.

176. Black, Jeremy. "Omitted from the Record: The Duke of Newcastle's Reassurance over British Foreign Policy in 1727." *Archives* 21 (1994): 80-82.

The Duke's important letter to the 3rd Earl of Carlisle is severely truncated in the HMC Carlisle volume (163). Newcastle was deputizing for his fellow-Secretary Townshend, who was very ill at the time, and in his letter, printed in full here, explained Britain's strained relations with Spain.

177. *British Diplomatic Instructions.* J. F. Chance and L. Wickham Legge, eds. London: Royal Historical Society, 1922-1934.

Prints Newcastle letters to diplomats in Denmark (v.36) and France (v.38, 43, 49) in 1720s-1740s.

178. Graham, John Murray. *Annals and Correspondence of the Viscount and the First and Second Earls of Stair.* Edinburgh: Blackwood, 1875. 2 vols.

Newcastle letters to John Dalrymple, the 2nd Earl, in 1731, 1733, 1734, and 1743 about appointments are printed in v.2. The Stair correspondence in general is useful on Scots affairs in the first half of the century.

179. Coxe, William. *Memoirs of Horatio, Lord Walpole.* London: Longman, 1820. 3rd ed., corrected and enlarged. 2 vols.

Walpole, younger brother of Sir Robert, was the Pelhams' friend and political ally. V.2 (1740-1757) includes several letters from Pelham and a few from Newcastle, chiefly on foreign affairs, which are listed by subject in the index.

180. *Private Correspondence of Chesterfield and Newcastle, 1744-1746.* Sir Richard Lodge, ed. Camden Society ser.3 v.44. London: Royal Historical Society, 1930.

Letters exchanged while Chesterfield was ambassador at the Hague and Lord Lieutenant in Dublin. Lodge's introduction puts the letters in context and explains why Chesterfield agreed to become Newcastle's fellow Secretary of State in 1746. These letters also throw light on London politics and relations between the Pelham brothers. See the Stanhope Papers (139).

181. *The Albemarle Papers.* Charles Terry, ed. Aberdeen: New Spalding Club, 1902. 2 vols.

Correspondence of William Keppel, 2nd Earl of Albemarle, about the Jacobite uprising 1746-1747 includes three letters from Newcastle and many to him from Albemarle and Andrew Fletcher, Lord Justice-Clerk of Scotland.

182. *Briefwisseling en Aanteekeningen van Willem Bentinck, Heer van Rhoon.* C. Gerretson and P. Geyl, eds. Utrecht: Kemink, 1934.

Prints the Dutch Count Bentinck's correspondence from the Egerton Manuscripts and the Newcastle Papers 1736-1748 and includes six Newcastle letters 1747-1748 about Anglo-Dutch relations at a difficult stage of the war.

183. *Correspondence of John, Fourth Duke of Bedford.* Lord John Russell, ed. London: Longman, 1842-1846. 3 vols.

Bedford, sometimes an ally of the Pelhams and sometimes an opponent, led the Admiralty 1744-1748 and was Southern Secretary 1748-1751. His correspondence covers 1742-1770, with fewer letters at the end. Well edited but omits portions of some letters and does not print every letter in the manuscript collection. In v.1 (to 1748), 43 Newcastle letters and nine Pelham letters; v.2 (to 1760), eight Newcastle letters; v.3, 14 Newcastle letters.

184. *Letters to Henry Fox, Lord Holland, with a Few Addressed to His Brother Stephen, Earl of Ilchester.* Earl of Ilchester, ed. London: Roxburghe Club, 1915.

Prints Pelham letters to Fox 1743 (2) and 1745 and to Ilchester 1746 and Newcastle letters to Fox 1748 and 1756 (2), copied from the Holland House Papers (50). This volume, which covers 1743-1770, also includes correspondence with almost every other prominent politician.

185. Cross, Arthur. *The Anglican Episcopate and the American Colonies.* New York: Longmans, 1902.

Prints Newcastle's correspondence 1749-1750 with Thomas Sherlock, Bishop of London, and Horatio Walpole about the possibility of appointing bishops for the American colonies.

186. *Memoirs and Papers of Sir Andrew Mitchell, K.B.* Andrew Bisset, ed. London: Chapman and Hall, 1850. 2 vols.

Mitchell was ambassador to Berlin 1756-1771. His early correspondence is useful on Scottish affairs, and the later, on relations with Prussia. Prints a Pelham letter 1747 and Newcastle letters 1747, 1752, 1756 (2), 1757, 1767.

187. *Memorials of the Public Life and Character of the Right Hon. James Oswald of Dunnikier.* Edinburgh: Constable, 1825.

Oswald served on the Treasury Board. His correspondence is useful on Scottish and opposition politics and includes letters from Grenville, Legge, and Dunk Halifax. Prints a Pelham letter 1751 about a place for Oswald and a Newcastle letter 1755 announcing appointments.

188. *Correspondence of William Pitt, Earl of Chatham.* W. S. Taylor and J. H. Pringle, eds. London: Murray, 1838. 4 vols.

These letters contain much important commentary on the Pelhams' relations with Pitt and his allies. In v.1-2 are two Pelham letters 1750, 32 Newcastle letters 1748-1764, and nine Pitt letters to the Duke 1747-1764.

189. *A Selection from the Papers of the Earls of Marchmont.* Sir George Rose, ed. London: Murray, 1831. 3 vols.

Marchmont's diary (v.1) for July 1744-March 1748 includes many comments about the Pelhams. Letters (1733-1750) in v.2, chiefly between opposition politicians, include a Newcastle letter 1747 and a Pelham letter 1750.

190. *Memoirs and Correspondence of George, Lord Lyttleton from 1734 to 1773.* Robert Phillimore, ed. London: Ridgway, 1845. 2 vols.

Prints letters from many politicians and writers, such as Chesterfield, Thomson, and Pope. Includes Pelham letters in v.1: 1747 (2) on elections and 1748 (2) on patronage. Pitt and Lyttelton letters after 1754 provide a good commentary on Newcastle's politics.

191. Wyndham, Maud. *Chronicles of the Eighteenth Century.* London: Hodder and Stoughton, 1924. 2 vols.

Reproduces letters of the Lyttelton family, their Grenville and West cousins,

Pitt, and other contemporaries. The narrative provides political context but is out of date. Most letters are truncated. Includes in v. 2 a Pelham letter 1751 on foreign affairs and Newcastle letters to George Lyttelton 1755 (2) congratulating him on his reelection and about his differences with Pitt over conduct of the war and 1760 on peace prospects and the 1761 supplies.

192. *The Grenville Papers.* William James Smith, ed. London: Murray, 1852-1853. 4 vols.

Correspondence 1742-1777 among the Cobham group contains important information on the Pelhams, including George Grenville's diary (1763 onward) in v.2-3. Printed in v.1 are Pelham letters 1748 and 1749 to Grenville and six Newcastle letters to Temple (1749, 1758, 1760) and one to Grenville (1761).

193. *Selections from the Family Papers Preserved at Caldwell.* W. Mure, ed. Glasgow: Eadie, 1854. 3 vols.

Political commentary from the Scots' view includes many letters from Bute. A Pelham letter (circular whip 1753) is printed in v.1.

194. Falkiner, C. Litton. "Correspondence of Archbishop Stone and the Duke of Newcastle." *English Historical Review* 20 (1905): 508-542 and 735-763.

George Stone's brother Andrew was Newcastle's Assistant Secretary. These well-annotated letters were written 1752-1758, while the Archbishop headed the Commission of Lord Justices in Ireland. Falkiner provides a brief introduction on Ireland and Stone's office. These letters throw light on Irish affairs, especially its Parliament, and London's policy toward Ireland.

195. *Memoirs of the Marquis of Rockingham and his Contemporaries.* Earl of Albemarle, ed. London: Bentley, 1852. 2 vols.

This history (from 1760) of a close political ally contains extensive quotations from Newcastle's letters. The editor says the Duke's "talents were not sufficiently appreciated" and were "far above mediocrity." Very perceptive on Pitt's faults.

196. Schweizer, Karl. "Lord Bute and British Strategy in the Seven Years War: Further Evidence." *Notes and Queries* 236 (1991): 189-191.

Prints a Newcastle letter 1761 to Hardwicke in which he expresses his fear that Bute planned to end British involvement in the continental war.

197. *Correspondence of King George III from 1760 to December 1783.* Sir John Fortescue, ed. London: Macmillan, 1927-1928. 6 vols.

V.1 contains useful reports on Newcastle's activities and two 1766 letters from him about his resignation and a clerical appointment.

198. Namier, Sir Lewis. *Additions and Corrections to Sir John Fortescue's Edition of the Correspondence of George the Third (Vol. I)*. Manchester: Manchester University Press, 1937.

Points out a host of errors in transcription and dating.

199. *A Narrative of the Changes in the Ministry 1765-1767*. Mary Bateson, ed. Camden Society n.s. v.59. London, Longmans, 1898.

Newcastle's letters (1c) to his friend John White, M.P., describing the brief Rockingham administration and the succeeding Chatham ministry. See McCahill (456).

200. *Correspondence of the Right Honourable Edmund Burke*. Earl Fitzwilliam and Sir Richard Bourke, eds. London: Rivington, 1844. 4 vols.

Newcastle's letter to Burke in August 1767 about the political situation is printed in v.1, p. 144.

201. *The Private Correspondence of David Garrick*. James Boaden, ed. London: Colburn and Bentley, 1831-1832. 2 vols.

Newcastle's letter of September 1767 to Garrick thanking him for the present of a horse is printed in v.1, p. 130.

3

Contemporary Memoirs, Diaries, and Correspondence Containing Important Material on the Pelhams

Letters written by friends or enemies of the Pelhams are a window on their activities, but the glass may be obscured by the writer's interpretation of events. Consequently, comparison of various accounts of the same event is a wise measure. Diaries are equally suspect but are more likely to reflect the writer's true feelings. Memoirs intended for publication and written years after events occurred may be the truth, to the best of the writer's recollection, or mere ax-grinding. The sources listed in this chapter should be used with the caution that the writers in their accounts may unconsciously (or purposely in the case of Horace Walpole) mislead the reader.

202. Walpole, Horace. *Memoirs of King George II*. John Brooke, ed. New Haven: Yale University Press, 1985. 3 vols.

203. Walpole, Horace. *Memoirs of the Reign of King George the Third*. G. F. Russell Barker, ed. Freeport, NY: Books for Libraries Press, 1970 reprint of 1894 ed. 2 vols.

204. *The Yale Edition of Horace Walpole's Correspondence*. W. S. Lewis et al., eds. New Haven: Yale University Press, 1937-1983. 48 vols.

One of the earliest sources available, Walpole's memoirs provided a convenient but distorted picture of the Pelhams. Nevertheless, used with care, the memoirs and Walpole's letters are a rich and invaluable source on the period. Walpole's malicious character sketches of the Pelhams and their ally Hardwicke are most accessible in *Horace Walpole: Memoirs and Portraits*, edited by Matthew Hodgart (New York: Macmillan, 1963). An explanation of Walpole's hostility to Newcastle can be found in George L. Lam, "Walpole and the Duke of Newcastle" in Warren H. Smith, ed., *Horace Walpole: Writer, Politician, and*

Connoisseur (New Haven: Yale University Press, 1967), pp. 57-84. For Walpole's secret attack on the Pelhams' administration on behalf of the Prince of Wales, see Romney Sedgwick, "Horace Walpole's Political Articles 1747-49" in Smith, pp. 45-55. See also Clark's introduction to Waldegrave (218) and Ian Christie, "Horace Walpole: The Gossip as Historian" (*History Today* 4 [1954]: 291-300).

205. *The Complete Works of Sir John Vanbrugh, Fourth Volume: The Letters.* Geoffrey Webb, ed. London: Nonesuch Press, 1928.

Prints Vanbrugh's letters to Newcastle 1715-1724, primarily about his renovations of Claremont and Newcastle House, but also containing in passing information about the Duke's activities. The architect's letters about his quarrel with the Duchess of Marlborough include information about his negotiating the Newcastle marriage (especially pp. 91-93).

206. Black, Jeremy. "The Papers of British Diplomats, 1689-1793." *Archives* 20 (1992): 225-253; "Appendix I." *Archives* 20 (1993): 213-218; "Appendix II." *Archives* 21 (1994): 205-213.

These articles provide important information about the content and location of papers of diplomats who corresponded with Newcastle.

207. *The Parliamentary Diary of Sir Edward Knatchbull 1722-1730,* A. N. Newman, ed. Camden Society 3rd ser. v.94. London: Royal Historical Society, 1963.

This diary contains many quotations from speeches by Pelham, then Secretary at War. Newman adds notes comparing reports on the same debates taken from other manuscripts.

208. *Manuscripts of the Earl of Egmont: Diary of Viscount Percival.* (HMC Report 63, pt. 2) London: HMSO, 1920-1923. 3 vols.

John Percival, later 1st Earl of Egmont, was a very able opposition speaker and writer. His diary (1729-1748) contains many references to the Pelhams' activities in Parliament.

209. Black, Jeremy. "New Light on the Session of 1729: Two Letters of Thomas Winnington." *Archives* 19 (1991): 297-305.

These letters provide more information than do the Knachtbull and Egmont diaries about debates in March on the Address and Army estimates and in April on Spanish attacks on British commerce.

210. Hervey, John, Lord Hervey. *Some Materials Towards Memoirs of the Reign of King George II.* Romney Sedgwick, ed. London: Eyre and Spottiswoode, 1931. 3 vols.

A favorite at Court for his sharp wit, Hervey despised the Pelhams. His political diary, which he kept 1733-1742, is valuable but highly prejudiced and so must be used with care.

211. *Recueil des Instructions données aux Ambassadeurs et Ministres de France: Bd. XXV, 2, Angleterre, Bd. 3 (1698-1791)*. Paul Vaucher, ed. Paris: Editions du Centre National, 1965.

Besides references to the Pelhams, these instructions include an assessment of Newcastle by a French minister written in 1737 and sketches of both brothers' characters in instructions for Mirepoix written in 1749.

212. Black, Jeremy. "Archival Sources for the Parliamentary History of Britain in the 1740s." *Archives* 19 (1991): 404-422.

Long quotations about Commons debates from the Tucker Papers and Campbell Papers include information on Pelham's speeches.

213. *The Commons Journal of Philip Yorke, 1743-1750*. Richard Connors, ed. Woodbridge: Boydell & Brewer, 1998.

Hardwicke's eldest son, usually identified by his courtesy title Lord Royston, knew more than did most of his fellow Members about the Pelhams' plans and goals. In consequence, his record of debates and observations about his colleagues are especially valuable. The manuscript is in the Hardwicke Papers (2o).

214. Glover, Richard. *Memoirs by a Celebrated Literary and Political Character*. London: Murray, 1814.

Glover was not only a poet but also a London merchant elected to Commons. His observations on politics 1742-1757 are not always reliable factually and generally are hostile to the Pelhams.

215. *The Political Journal of George Bubb Dodington*. John Carswell and L. A. Dralle, eds. Oxford: Clarendon Press, 1965.

A political hack with some electoral influence, Dodington was a member of the Leicester House opposition until his patron's death in 1751. Despite his jaundiced view of the Pelhams, Dodington then solicited places from them.

216. *Report on Manuscripts in Various Collections, Volume VI*. London: HMSO, 1909.

Dodington's correspondence in the Eyre Matcham Papers is useful on the Pelhams.

217. Garnett, Richard. "Correspondence of Archbishop Herring and Lord

Hardwicke during the Rebellion of 1745." *English Historical Review* 19 (1904): 528-550 and 719-742.

These letters are taken from the Hardwicke Papers (35598) and cover September 1745-January 1746. They provide both a narrative of events and insight into the ministry's reactions to events and plans to combat the rebellion.

218.   *The Memoirs and Speeches of James, 2nd Earl Waldegrave, 1742-1763.* J.C.D. Clark, ed. Cambridge: Cambridge University Press, 1988.

Waldegrave was a friend of both Pelhams, and his memoirs provide insight into their relations with the Young Court around Prince George. Clark's introduction and annotations are excellent.

219.   *Archives ou Correspondence inédite de la Maison d'Orange-Nassau.* Th. Bussemaker, ed. 4th series. Leyden: Sijthoff, 1908-1917. 4 vols.

These volumes are made up primarily of the correspondence of Dutch Count Willem Bentinck. He reported conversations with the Pelhams in London 1747-1751 (v.1-2) and commented on Newcastle's activities 1756-1766 (v.3-4).

220.   Barrow, Sir John. *The Life of George Lord Anson.* London: Murray, 1839.

This uncritical biography of the rightly famous admiral reproduces, not always accurately, letters about naval affairs and politics from Anson, Hardwicke, Bedford, Sandwich, and other contemporaries, written mainly in the 1740s and 1750s.

221.   Lawson, Philip. "Further Reflections on the Cabinet in the Early Years of George III's Reign." *Bulletin of the Institute for Historical Research* 57 (1984): 237-240.

Points out reports in the Grenville Papers of Cabinet meetings held in 1748, 1757, 1760, and 1762, which provide insight into the conduct of business.

222.   *Additional Grenville Papers, 1763-1765.* J.R.G. Tomlinson, ed. Manchester: Manchester University Press, 1962.

These thoroughly annotated letters contain many references to Newcastle's activities in opposition. To assist researchers, Tomlinson provides an explanation of how and why the Grenville Papers are divided among various repositories.

223.   *An Eighteenth Century Correspondence.* Lilian Dickens and Mary Stanton, eds. London: Murray, 1910.

Letters to architect Sanderson Miller from Pitt, the Lytteltons, the Grenvilles,

Charles Jenkinson, and other contemporaries containing comments on the political scene. The volume is well edited.

224. *The Diary of Thomas Turner 1754-1765.* David Vaisey, ed. Oxford: Oxford University Press, 1984.

Turner was a shopkeeper in East Hoathly, Sussex, near the Pelham family estate Halland, and included many comments about Newcastle's activities in his diary. This thoroughly annotated and illustrated edition contributes to an understanding of the Duke's county patronage.

225. *Letters from George III to Lord Bute 1756-1766.* Romney Sedgwick, ed. London: Macmillan, 1939.

These fully annotated letters written to his mentor show how George's dependence on Bute lessened as his self-confidence grew. They also reveal the young king's long-standing animosity to Newcastle.

226. *The Devonshire Diary, 1759-1762.* Peter Brown and Karl Schweizer, eds. London: Royal Historical Society, 1982.

Newcastle's close associate Devonshire wrote this account of the often rancorous relations within the ministry during the changes in reign. Useful on Newcastle's gradual loss of influence.

227. Schweizer, Karl. "Some Additions to the Devonshire Diary." *Notes and Queries* 231 (1986): 64-67.

Devonshire made notes on his conversations with George II and Cumberland in 1757 concerning the Convention of Klosterseven. Appended are character assessments of several contemporaries, including the Pelham brothers, possibly copied rather than written by Devonshire.

228. Fox, Henry (1st Baron Holland). "Memoir on the Events Attending the Death of George II and the Accession of George III" in Countess of Ilchester and Lord Stavordale, eds., *The Life and Letters of Lady Sarah Lennox*, pp. 3-81. London: Murray, 1904.

Fox expected to succeed Pelham as Leader of Commons in 1754 and became a bitter and frustrated politician when he did not. His remembrances of the events of 1760-1763 are colored by his resentment of Newcastle.

229. Schweizer, Karl. "A Lost Letter of John Stuart, 3rd Earl of Bute, to George Grenville, 13th October 1761." *Historical Journal* 17 (1974): 435-442.

Bute dismissed Newcastle as "this feeble old man" unable to oppose or influence

George III and condemned the Duke as a poor administrator and weak Secretary but said he had acted fairly to Bute.

230. *The Jenkinson Papers, 1760-1766.* N. S. Jucker, ed. London: Macmillan, 1949.

Secretary to both Bute and Grenville, rising young politician Charles Jenkinson recorded his acute comments on political events.

231. *The Correspondence of Edmund Burke.* Thomas Copeland, ed. Chicago: University of Chicago Press, 1958-1978. 10 vols.

Burke's reply to Newcastle's August 1767 letter is printed in v.1. Other letters in v.1 and 2, especially those between Burke and Rockingham, include many references to the Duke's political activities.

4

Speeches in Parliament

Neither brother had a reputation as a great speaker, but Pelham spoke strongly against a motion to remove Walpole in February 1741 and Newcastle was effective in the debate over repeal of the Stamp Act in March 1766. Both were administrators throughout their careers and, in consequence, spoke often and on important issues. After the fall of Walpole and Carteret, each Pelham became Leader of his House, organizing support for their program in debate. Newcastle often called on his friend Hardwicke, an excellent speaker, for support.

Although reporting of speeches in Parliament by the press was prohibited, some newspapers and magazines printed thinly disguised accounts. Since most speeches were not recorded in the *Journals*, those found in the following volumes were put together from many sources, such as letters, diaries, and memoirs, and cannot be considered literal reports.

232. Cobbett, William. *The Parliamentary History of England*. London: Hansard, 1806-1820. 36 vols.

The most commonly available work but not as accurate or complete as Almon and Debrett. See v.7-15 for speeches by both Pelhams. A rough index is printed at the front of each volume. Available on microfilm from the Center for Research Libraries, Chicago.

233. Chandler, Richard. *The History and Proceedings of the House of Commons from the Restoration to the Present Time*. London: Printed for Chandler, 1742-44. 14 vols.

Pelham's speeches can be found in v.6-14 (1714-1740). A speakers' index is printed in each volume.

234.   Almon, John. *Debates and Proceedings of the British House of Commons from 1743 to 1774*. London: Printed for Almon, 1766-1775. 11 vols. Incorporated into *The History, Debates and Proceedings of both Houses of Parliament, 1743 to 1774*. London: John Debrett, 1792. 7 vols.

See v.1-5 (1743-1754) of Almon for Pelham's speeches. A list of speakers at front of each volume is the only index. Microfilm of Debrett is available from the Center for Research Libraries, Chicago.

235.   Timberland, Ebenezer. *The History and Proceedings of the House of Lords from the Restoration in 1660*. London: Timberland, 1742-43. 8 vols.

Newcastle's speeches can be found in v.3-8 (1714-1742). The table of contents is the only index.

236.   Torbuck, John. *A Collection of the Parliamentary Debates in England*. London: Torbuck, 1739-1743. 20 vols.

Speeches by both Pelhams can be found in v.7-20. The table of contents is the only index.

237.   Stock, Leo, ed. *Proceedings and Debates of the British Parliaments Respecting North America*. Washington, D.C.: Carnegie Institution, 1924-1941. 5 vols.

These volumes contain only material relating to North America extracted from the *Journals* and committee reports. V.3 (1930) covers 1702-1727; v.4 (1937), 1728-1739; v.5 (1941), 1739-1754.

238.   Simmons, R. C., and P.D.G. Thomas, eds. *Proceedings and Debates of the British Parliaments Respecting North America, 1754-1783*. London: Kraus, 1982-1987. 6 vols.

Brings together reports from diaries, correspondence, and the *Journals*. V.1 (1982) covers 1754-1764; v.2 (1982), 1765-1768.

239.   The Center for Research Libraries, Chicago, holds microfilm of the House of Lords *Journals* and *Sessional Papers* and the House of Commons *Journals* and the microprint Readex set of the Commons *Sessional Papers* (also called Parliamentary Papers). Chadwyck-Healey has microfilmed *Reports from Committees of the House of Commons*

1715-1801 printed but not inserted in the Journals of the House and published a facsimile of its *General Index*. The *Reports* were originally published in 16 volumes in 1803-1806.

240. Torrington, F. W., ed. *House of Lords Sessional Papers 1726-1805.* Dobbs Ferry, NY: Oceana, 1972-1978. 58 vols.

The papers are reprinted in photographic facsimile from the original printed documents.

241. Lambert, Sheila, ed. *House of Commons Sessional Papers of the Eighteenth Century.* Wilmington: Scholarly Resources, 1975-1976. 145 vols.

The set covers 1715-1800, with the bulk of the material from the later part of the century. The introduction (v.1) explains the different types of documents (bills, reports, and papers) and their history. The documents are listed by date: 1701-1760, v.1, and 1761-1800, v.2. V.3-21 cover documents for the Pelham era (to 1768), although reports and papers of later date, even from the nineteenth century, can contain data from the earlier period.

242. Lambert, Sheila, ed. *List & Index Society Special Series Volume 1: List of House of Commons Sessional Papers 1701-1750* (London: Swift, 1968).

The following are useful guides for research into the Pelhams' activities in Parliament:

243. Bond, Maurice. *Guide to the Records of Parliament*. London: HMSO, 1971.

Lists classes of records for both Houses and gives detailed information on each class.

244. Menhennet, David. *The Journal of the House of Commons: A Bibliographical and Historical Guide*. London: HMSO, 1971.

Sections on the history and indexing of the *Journal* are useful. A section on contents uses modern examples, making it less helpful.

245. Jones, David Lewis. *Debates and Proceedings of the British Parliaments: A Guide to Printed Sources*. London: HMSO, 1986.

This volume covers the English, British, Irish, and Scottish parliaments. Jones gives the history of reporting of parliamentary activities and names journals in which reports appeared. See p. 49 for the eighteenth century. Lists of sources for each period are provided.

246. *A Bibliography of Parliamentary Debates of Great Britain*. House of Commons Library Document No. 2. London: HMSO, 1956.

See for lists and evaluations of various editions of debates, diaries, and proceedings.

247. Ford, Percy and Grace. *A Guide to Parliamentary Papers*. Shannon: Irish University Press, 1972. 3rd ed.

Describes the Papers and their history and tells how to find and use them.

248. Rodgers, Frank, and Rose Phelps. *A Guide to British Parliamentary Papers*. Urbana: University of Illinois Graduate School of Library Science, 1967 (Occasional Paper No. 82).

Gives the history of the *Journals* and sessional papers and explains how to use the microprint Readex set of the latter. The authors also list many reference works for eighteenth-century papers.

249. Ditchfield, G. M., David Hayton, and Clyve Jones, eds. *British Parliamentary Lists, 1660-1800: A Register*. London: Hambledon, 1995.

Division lists of how Lords and Commoners voted on questions and bills were compiled by individuals and were not printed in the *Journals*. Many for the Pelham era survive in the Newcastle Papers and are listed in this volume, which gives all information needed to find and understand each list.

250. Ginter, Donald, ed. *Voting Records of the British House of Commons, 1761-1820*. London: Hambledon, 1995. 6 vols.

Newcastle's influence was already waning in 1761, and he had only seven more years to live. Nevertheless, these volumes provide information about his young friends who formed the nucleus of the Rockingham Whigs. V.1 includes a handlist and sources for the voting records. Biographical listings of Members are given in v.2, A-F, v.3, G-O, and v.4, P-Z. The divisions are chronicled in v.5, 1761-1809, and v.6, 1810-1820.

5

Pamphlets Relating to the Pelhams

The Pelhams' long service in office elicited wide-spread praise and condemnation in pamphlets, newspapers, journals, and periodicals, most heavily after 1740. Privately issued pamphlets were the favorite vehicle for presenting arguments on political issues and were aimed at an educated audience willing to pay for them. The authors could be aroused citizens, members of the administration, opposition politicians, or journalists hired to produce propaganda. Pamphlets referring to the Pelhams are listed in the *National Union Catalogue* and *British Library Catalogue* and in Robert Watt, *Bibliotheca Britannica* (New York: Franklin, 1965 reprint of 1824 ed.). See also Charles Evans, *American Bibliography: A Chronological Dictionary of all Books, Pamphlets and Periodical Publications from 1639 to 1820* (New York: Smith, 1941 reprint of 1903 ed.), 13 vols. The Evans work has been published as a Readex microprint set, available from the Center for Research Libraries, Chicago. Many pamphlets have been microfilmed for the British Library's on-going project The Eighteenth Century Short Title Catalogue. The microfilm is published by Research Publications Inc., Woodbridge, CT, together with a printed guide. *The Eighteenth Century: Guide to the Microform Collection* is updated as new reels are issued. Some larger university libraries own this collection, and, in the United States, the index is accessible through the Research Libraries Information Network (RLIN) on-line data base.

Lists of pamphlets relevant to particular periods and topics can be found in Brewer (571), Browning (569), Clark (433), Eldon (507), Foord (362), Harding (493), Nulle (316), Peters (437), Perry (375), Harris (298), Schlenke (423), Dickson (378), and Wilkes (319).

References to the Pelhams occur in too many pamphlets to list all of them here. The following are either about or addressed to the brothers:

251.   *The state of the case between the Lord Chamberlain and Sir R. Steele as represented by that knight. Restated in vindication of King George and the...Duke of Newcastle.* 1720.

252.   *Reasons humbly offered for buying and selling in the army. In a letter to the Secretary at War* [Pelham]. 1725.

253.   *Robin-Hood and the Duke of Lancaster: A ballad.* [Sir Robert Walpole and Newcastle.] 1727.

254.   Horatius Flaccus (pseud.). *The Fifth Ode of the First Book of Horace imitated.* [A lampoon on Newcastle.] 1745.

255.   *A Letter to the most noble Thomas, Duke of Newcastle, on certain points of the last importance to these nations.* 1746.

256.   *Power and Patriotism: a poetical epistle...to...H. P.* 1746.

257.   *Remarks upon a Letter (just made publick) on certain points...to...Newcastle.* 1746.

258.   *Mr. P--m's Speech immediately before his execution.* [A satire.] 1747.

259.   Hughes, Michael. *A Letter to the most noble Thomas, Duke of Newcastle, on the dangers arising from Popery and Disaffection.* 1747.

260.   *The Puppet Shew: a poem humbly inscribe to H___ P___.* [Political satire.] 1748.

261.   *The Finesse of Rantum Scantum, a...dialogue betwixt Tom and Harry, Fratres fraterrimi.* 1748.

262.   *A Tale of Two Tubs, or the B---s in Querpo.* London: Price, 1749. Printed in part in Nulle (289).

263.   *An Examination of the Principles and an enquiry into the conduct of the two B***rs.* 1749.

264.   *The Conduct of the two B***rs vindicated.* 1749.

265.   *A second series of Facts and Arguments tending to prove that the abilities of the two B--rs are not more extraordinary than their virtues.* 1749.

266. *An Ode for the Thanksgiving Day.* [Satire on Peace of 1749.] ?1749.

267. Mason, W. *Ode performed...at Cambridge...at the Installation of...New-castle.* 1749.

268. *An occasional Letter to the Right Honourable H--- P---, Esq.* 1750.

269. *A Fragment.* [Satire on Newcastle's election as Chancellor of Cambridge.] ?1750.

270. *Proposals to the Legislature for preventing the frequent executions and exportations of convicts. In a letter to H. Pelham.* 1754.

271. Merryfellow, Richard (pseud.). *A letter to John Shadwell...with observations...occasion'd by the death of the Rt. Hon. H--y P--m, Esq.* 1754.

272. *The Block and Yard Arm. A...ballad on the loss of Minorca.* [Attack on Newcastle.] 1756.

273. *A serious call to the Corporation of London to address his M---y to remove from his councils...weak and wicked M---s.* [Attack on Newcastle's administration.] 1756.

274. *The Wonder of Surry!...being a true and faithful narrative of what passed between an oak and a certain great minister* [Newcastle]. ?1756.

275. *The Resignation, or, The fox out of the pit and the geese in, with B--g at the bottom.* 1756.

276. *Birds for the Tower.* [Ballad on Newcastle's conduct toward Byng.] ?1756.

277. *A Letter to the University of Cambridge on the late resignation* [of Newcastle from office]. 1756.

278. *The Levee: a poem. Occasion'd by the number of clergy at the Duke of Ne---le's last levee.* 1756.

279. *A Dream. Note, Satan gave this advice to Sir Bobbity Blue String* [Newcastle]. 1756.

280. *The Enquiry is not begun.* [Satire on Newcastle.] 1757.

281. *A full and particular account of a...dreadful...apparition which appeared to a certain Great Man* [Byng's ghost and Newcastle]. ?1757.

282. *Past twelve o'clock, or Byng's Ghost.* [Satire on Newcastle.] 1757.

283. *If Justice is begun? Let it continue.* [Attack on Newcastle administration.] ?1757.

284. *A Letter to His Grace the D___ of N___e on the duty he owes himself, his King, his Country and his God at this important moment.* 1757.

285. *Courtier and Patriot. An epistle to...the Duke of Newcastle.* London: Woodfall, ?1757.

286. *An ode inscribed to the triumvirate; more particularly his Grace of N***.* London: Scott, 1757.

287. *The Cries of the Public. In a Letter to the Duke of Newcastle.* 1758.

288. *A Letter addressed to Two Great Men on the prospect of peace.* 1760.

289. *The Right Honourable annuitant vindicated. With a word or two in favour of the other great man, in case of his resignation.* [Satire on Pitt and Newcastle.] 1761.

290. *A Letter to His Grace the Duke of N**** on the present Crisis.* 1761.

291. *An Address to the City of London* [defending Newcastle]. 1762.

292. *The Coalition: or an Historical Memorial of the Negotiation for Peace between His High Mightiness of C-m-t and His Sublime Excellency of H-y-s* [Newcastle and Pitt]. 1762.

293. *An ode, sacred to the memory of a late eminently distinguish'd placeman on his retiring from business.* 1763.

6

Newspapers

By the 1740s, when the Pelhams formed their administration, newspapers were an important source of information, carrying foreign and domestic news, advertising, and editorials commenting on the political scene, although direct reporting of debates in Parliament was prohibited. The *London Gazette* was the official government newspaper in the Pelham era. Information about its operation can be found in Thomson (391). Country weeklies and London dailies reached even the illiterate, who would gather round while a friend read out the articles. The London papers were especially influencial and rarely impartial. Most favored a particular political viewpoint, and some were financed by administration or opposition supporters. Consequently, newspapers, like pamphlets, must be treated as sources of opinion rather than facts about the Pelhams. Marie Peters ably addressed this question in "Historians and the Eighteenth-Century English Press: A Review of Possibilities and Problems" (*Australian Journal of Politics and History* 34 [1988]: 37-50).

294. *Early English Newspapers.* Microfilm set issued by Research Publications and held by a number of university libraries.

This set reproduces the Burney Collection held by the British Library and the Nichols Collection held by the Bodleian Library, Oxford, which together include most papers of the period. While the Burney Collection is bound chronologically, the microfilm is assembled by title. Lists of titles and information on individual newspapers can be found in Cornish (592) and Schweizer (593)

295. *Foreign Newspapers Held by the Center for Research Libraries.* Chicago: CRL, 1992. 2 vols.

This catalogue lists holdings of eighteenth-century British papers available for loan on microfilm. Check listings in the latest edition of *Guide to Microforms in Print* (Munich: Saur, 1996) to find microfilm of papers which has become available since this catalogue was issued.

Information about contemporary newspapers can be found in the *Journal of Newspaper and Periodical History* and *Publishing History* and in the following:

296.   Harris, Michael. *London Newspapers in the Age of Walpole: A Study of the Origins of the Modern English Press*. London: Associated University Presses, 1987.

Harris provides an overview of finance, distribution, and content of the papers. His section on political control of the press is useful on Newcastle.

297.   Black, Jeremy. *The English Press in the Eighteenth Century*. London: Croom Helm, 1987.

This work covers more aspects of press influence than Harris (296) but is less useful on Newcastle because of its broader time-frame.

298.   Harris, Robert. *A Patriot Press: National Politics and the London Press in the 1740s*. Oxford: Clarendon Press, 1993.

Harris looks at the press as an expression of public opinion and political views, especially in reaction to the War of the Austrian Succession. He notes changes in press reaction year by year. Tory-Patriot pamphlets are listed in an appendix.

299.   Crane, R. S., and F. B. Kaye. *A Census of British Newspapers and Periodicals 1620-1800*. London: Holland Press, 1966 rev. ed.

This volume is rather old but still useful for beginning a search. It lists British periodicals held by American libraries and those not held in the U.S. The authors provide information on the publishing history, editors, and contributors of the publications listed.

300.   Hanson, Laurence. *Government and the Press 1695-1763*. London: Oxford University Press, 1936.

An old but still useful examination of the history of press law and newspaper stamp taxes and administration of the law. Hanson includes a long chapter on the government paper, the *London Gazette*.

301.   Peters, Marie. "The Monitor, 1755-1765: A Political Essay Paper and Popular London Opinion." Ph.D. thesis, University of Canterbury, New Zealand, 1974.

This newspaper supported Pitt as he fought his way to a coalition with Newcastle but had difficulty reconciling its Tory view with Pitt's subsequent actions and policies.

302. Rea, Robert. *The English Press in Politics, 1760-1774.* Lincoln: University of Nebraska Press, 1963.

Useful on Newcastle's part in the 1760s press war.

303. Spector, R. D. *Political Controversy: A Study of Eighteenth-Century Propaganda.* New York: Greenwood, 1992.

This study examines a weekly newspaper that reprinted material from other papers together with its own editor's annotations and commentary. Useful on the 1760s propaganda war against Bute.

7

Journals and Periodicals

The popular magazines of the Pelham period usually appeared monthly and most often published a range of material in each issue, including poetry, book and pamphlet reviews or excerpts, political commentary, and letters to the editor. They provide insight into public opinion about the Pelhams. In addition to the British Library and Library of Congress, many large university libraries hold collections of the following best-known periodicals. Information on their editors and political viewpoints can be found in Cornish (592) and Schweizer (593). Many periodicals have been reproduced by University Microfilms and can be borrowed from the Center for Research Libraries, Chicago. See (312) for guides.

304. *Gentleman's Magazine*. Founded 1731.

305. *London Magazine*. Founded 1732.

306. *Scots Magazine*. Founded 1738.

307. *Universal Magazine*. Founded 1747.

308. *Monthly Review*. Founded 1749.

309. *Critical Review*. Founded 1756.

310. *Annual Register*. Founded 1758.

311. *British Magazine*. Founded 1759.

312. *British Periodicals, General and Literary ca.1660-1990*. Microfilm set held by the Center for Research Libraries, Chicago.

Two guides to this set have been published: *A Guide to the Early British Periodicals Collection on Microfilm with Title, Subject, Editor and Reel Number Indexes* and *Accessing English Literary Periodicals: A Guide to the Microfilm Collection, with Title, Subject, Editor and Reel Number Indexes*.

Information about magazines can be found in the following:

313.   Graham, Walter. *English Literary Periodicals*. New York: Octagon, 1966 reprint of 1930 ed.

Provides a brief overview of the development, political orientation, and content of periodicals.

314.   Bond, R. P., ed. *Studies in the Early English Periodical*. Chapel Hill: University of North Carolina Press, 1957.

Although only one political journal, the *World*, is included in these studies, Bond's introduction gives a useful overview of periodical history 1700-1760.

315.   Spector, R. D. *English Literary Periodicals and the Climate of Opinion During the Seven Years' War*. The Hague: Mouton, 1966.

Provides information on how various journals portrayed Newcastle.

8

The Pelhams' Lives and Careers

A. BIOGRAPHIES

All of the major biographies are 20 or more years old and do not go into the brothers' activities in office in any detail. Supplemental reading of newer studies of specific events or periods is essential for gaining a true picture of how well they succeeded professionally.

316. Nulle, Stebelton. *Thomas Pelham-Holles, Duke of Newcastle: His Early Political Career 1693-1724*. Philadelphia: University of Pennsylvania Press, 1931.

This thorough study by an admirer provides the most detailed information on family background, early life, and Sussex politics. Nulle says little about Newcastle's service as Lord Chamberlain, concentrating instead on the political ramifications of his marriage and his position within the Stanhope-Sunderland ministry. Appendices include a genealogical table of the Pelham and Holles families and a long quotation from the 1749 satirical poem *A Tale of Two Tubs, or the B[rother]s in Querpo.*

317. Browning, Reed. *The Duke of Newcastle*. New Haven: Yale University Press, 1975.

In this, the only full biography, Browning organizes his mass of sources by depicting Newcastle in his successive offices. The work is well-written and thoroughly indexed and paints a reasonably accurate portrait of the Duke. However, since recent studies indicate Newcastle was a more able minister than he previously was thought to be, this portrait is somewhat misleading. Browning disputes some figures used by Kelch (318) but otherwise agrees about the distressing story of the Duke's finances.

318. Kelch, Ray. *Newcastle, a Duke without Money: Thomas Pelham-Holles 1693-1768*. Berkeley: University of California Press, 1974.

This study of Newcastle's personal finances shows that his lavish life style and building expenditures rather than his electoral spending consumed his inheritance. Kelch offers an interesting analysis of the Duke's personality based on his spending patterns and presents considerable information about the Duchess and the Newcastles' private life gleaned from the financial records. Kelch and Browning (317) disagree on the size of the Duke's income.

319. Wilkes, John. *A Whig in Power: The Political Career of Henry Pelham*. Evanston: Northwestern University Press, 1964.

The only modern full-length biography, this work is inaccurate on some small details and misleading if not read with Browning (317) and Owen (347). The disappearance of a large portion of Pelham's papers hampers any researcher, but Wilkes' bibliography indicates he used most of the sources then available to flesh out his portrait. Pelham will always appear rather gray against his brother's vivid vitality. Wilkes is persuasive on Pelham's ability as an administrator and political manager and on his character and personality.

320. Coxe, William. *Memoirs of the Administration of the Right Honourable Henry Pelham*. London: Longman, 1829. 2 vols.

Written by the great Whig historian to refute Horace Walpole's memoirs (202), this work is based on Pelham's surviving papers, the Newcastle Papers, and seven other manuscript collections. Coxe made an unsuccessful search for papers reportedly held by Pelham's secretary. Coxe's command of sources and extensive use of quotations make this still the first resort for historians. See Paul Fritz, "Archdeacon William Coxe as Political Biographer" in Fritz and David Williams, eds., *The Triumph of Culture: 18th Century Perspectives* (Toronto: Hakkert, 1972), pp. 211-224.

321. Barnes, Donald. "Henry Pelham and the Duke of Newcastle." *Journal of British Studies* 1 (1962): 62-77.

Barnes believes the brothers "differed almost as much as two individuals can in temperament, character, and political opinions" and rates Pelham the superior politician.

322. Van Thal, Herbert, ed. *The Prime Ministers from Sir Robert Walpole to Edward Heath*. New York: Stein and Day, 1975.

The entries in this volume were written by well-qualified historians: Aubrey Newman on Pelham and H. T. Dickinson on Newcastle. Their accounts (pp. 59-91) are fairly accurate and balanced and explain the political context of the Pelhams' careers.

323. Englefield, Dermot, Janet Seaton, and Isobel White. *Facts About the British Prime Ministers*. New York: Wilson, 1995.

Entries for the Pelhams (pp. 11-22) bring together in compact form facts gathered from many sources but include errors such as saying Pelham died poor.

324. *The Dictionary of National Biography*. Various publishers and editions.

The original series was published by Smith, Elder & Co. in London in 1885-1901. The Pelham brothers' entries are well written but out of date. A new edition is in preparation and should be in print soon after the year 2000.

325. Pike, E. Royston. *Britain's Prime Ministers from Walpole to Wilson*. Feltham: Odhams Books, 1968.

The section on the Pelhams is primarily anecdotal, with mainly accurate dates and facts. Pike is surprisingly fair to Newcastle as finance minister by pointing out Pitt's extravagance.

326. Thomson, George Malcolm. *The Prime Ministers from Robert Walpole to Margaret Thatcher*. New York: Morrow, 1981.

This account of the Pelhams' lives and careers is brief and chiefly anecdotal, with most facts and dates correct, but Thomson misjudges Newcastle.

327. Bigham, Clive (2nd Viscount Mersey). *The Prime Ministers of Britain 1721-1921*. New York: Dutton, 1922.

The entries include many inaccuracies of fact, but Bigham's appraisal of the characters of the brothers is well done. He points out that Newcastle could not have stayed in office so long "without possessing considerable abilities."

B. EARLY LIFE, FAMILY, AND GENEALOGY

What little is known about the brothers' childhood and youth, together with their family background, can be found in Nulle (316), Browning (317), Kelch (318), Wilkes (319), and Coxe (320). Genealogies can be found in Nulle, Coxe,

Campbell (328), and Williams (394). Englefield (323) gives the most complete listing of siblings and children.

328.   Campbell, Peter, ed. *A House in Town: 22 Arlington Street, Its Owners and Builders*. London: Batsford, 1984.

This work about Pelham's townhouse includes a good bit of family history, an extensive genealogy (pp. 68-69), and a portrait of their father Baron Pelham (p. 66). It also covers the Pelhams as patrons of Sir John Vanbrugh, William Kent, and other architects and tells much about their lifestyle.

329.   McCormick, Frank. "Vanbrugh and the Duke of Newcastle: The Genesis of the Loverule Plot in *A Journey to London*." *Bulletin of Research in the Humanities* 86 (1983): 216-222.

The Duchess of Marlborough used the architect-playwright as a matchmaker between her granddaughter and Newcastle. Negotiations were protracted, McCormick believes, partly because of Harriet's lack of beauty and small dowry but mostly because of Newcastle's desire for a wife who would be not only a "useful and faithful Friend" but also "an Agreeable Companion." Vanbrugh said the Duke deplored "the bad education and wrong manners" of the young ladies at Court and despaired of finding a wife. The Duke, he said, "had thoughts about marriage not very usual with men of Great Quality and Fortune especially so young as he was." The marriage proved a great success, perhaps due to Newcastle's foresight. McCormick contends that a conversation about marriage in the play was based on Vanbrugh's with the Duke and that he abandoned the play rather than offend his wealthy patron.

C. EARLY CAREERS

While far more documentation survives for Newcastle than for Pelham before 1740, information about Pelham often is included in that documentation and consequently turns up in studies nominally about his brother.

330.   Howells, Catherine. "The Kit-Cat Club: A Study of Patronage and Influence in Britain, 1696-1720." Ph.D. thesis, University of California at Los Angeles, 1982.

The Club, which dissolved in 1720, began as weekly dinner meetings of writers and their patrons and became the Whig political center in the reign of Anne. Newcastle and Robert Walpole were among the prominent politicians who were members. This study examines how the Whig patrons got government appointments for these literati and how the Tories turned them out.

331. Hatton, Ragnhild. *George I, Elector and King.* Cambridge: Harvard University Press, 1978.

This excellent and only scholarly biography of the first Hanoverian monarch covers his fascinating family background and marriage, his role as absolute ruler of his beloved electorate, and his life as constitutional ruler of Great Britain. This study provides context for the Pelhams' early careers and includes many references to them.

332. Beattie, John M. *The English Court in the Reign of George I.* Cambridge: Cambridge University Press, 1967.

As Lord Chamberlain 1714-1724, Newcastle had charge of the largest department in the royal household. Beattie describes the structure, function, and finances of the household and provides much detailed information about how the Duke fulfilled his office.

333. Winton, Calhoun. *Sir Richard Steele, M.P.: The Later Career.* Baltimore: Johns Hopkins Press, 1970.

This volume explains how Steele's acquaintance with Newcastle began, the Duke's offer of the Boroughbridge seat to the writer for the 1715 general election, and their quarrel that eventually led to the closing of the Drury Lane theater.

334. Viator, Timothy. "Theobald's Preface to *Richard II* and the Possible Closing of Lincoln's Inn Fields in 1719." *Restoration and 18th Century Theatre Research* 3, #1 (1988): 30-33.

Inferences drawn from the theater manager's preface indicate Newcastle as Lord Chamberlain had already forced its closure before he closed Steele's Drury Lane theater in 1720. Both theaters were located close to the Duke's town house, a coincidence Viator does not examine.

335. Black, Jeremy. *Robert Walpole and the Nature of Politics in Early Eighteenth-Century Britain.* New York: St. Martin's Press, 1990.

This masterly summation of Walpole's career provides an excellent brief account of the political changes the Pelhams experienced before forming their own ministry.

336.   Coxe, William. *Memoirs of the Life and Administration of Sir Robert Walpole.* London: Cadell and Davies, 1798. 3 vols.

This history of the Pelhams' great patron throws light on their early careers and includes a perceptive character study of Newcastle. This first edition is the only one with a complete set of illustrative correspondence and papers (v.2-3). The 1800 edition has none, and the 1816 edition, only a selection from the correspondence but with new additions.

337.   Plumb, J. H. *Sir Robert Walpole: The King's Minister.* Boston: Houghton Mifflin, 1961.

Plumb never completed his biography of Walpole. This volume, the second, covers 1722-1734 and includes much information on the Pelhams' first years in politics.

338.   Nulle, S. H. "The Duke of Newcastle and the Election of 1727." *Journal of Modern History* 9 (1937): 1-22.

A study of Newcastle's first election as Secretary of State and for a new king. Nulle shows that the Duke's influence still lay mainly in Sussex, Nottingham, and his other properties but was being extended more widely.

339.   Black, Jeremy. "Fresh Light on the Fall of Townshend." *Historical Journal* 29 (1986): 41-64.

By 1728, Newcastle felt able to question Townshend's judgment on foreign policy, and this conflict led the Northern Secretary to seek the Duke's dismissal from office in 1729. Thwarted on this point, struggling with Walpole for authority in the ministry, and failing in his health, Townshend still had the King's support but resigned in 1730, apparently over these ministerial conflicts rather than over any dispute on foreign policy itself.

340.   Langford, Paul. *The Excise Crisis: Society and Politics in the Age of Walpole.* Oxford: Clarendon Press, 1975.

Walpole's attempt to reform the excise system in 1733 drew a most unfavorable public reaction and provided a political lesson for his deputy Pelham as they tried to gain passage of the bill. Langford explains the political situation and how members of Parliament reacted to the affair.

341.   Williams, Basil. "The Duke of Newcastle and the Election of 1734." *English Historical Review* 12 (1897): 448-488.

Williams draws an affectionate but not uncritical portrait of Newcastle as an efficient manager of the crucial election held after the Excise Crisis, giving details of the Duke's finances, patronage, and methods of campaigning.

342. Perkins, Clarence. "Electioneering in Eighteenth-Century England." *Quarterly Journal of the University of North Dakota* 13 (1923): 103-124.

This study examines Newcastle's expensive year-long campaign to control Sussex votes in the 1741 election.

343. Black, Jeremy. "The House of Lords and British Foreign Policy, 1720-48" in Clyve Jones, ed., *A Pillar of the Constitution: The House of Lords in British Politics, 1640-1784*, pp. 113-136. London: Hambledon Press, 1989.

An analysis of the influence of the House of Lords on the conduct of foreign policy. Since most Secretaries of State were peers, the Lords had ample opportunity to express their views face to face. Black quotes Newcastle and Hardwicke in debate.

344. Pemberton, W. Baring. *Carteret: The Brilliant Failure of the Eighteenth Century*. London: Longmans, 1936.

This work is the only modern biography, other than Williams (394), of the Pelhams' most able opponent in the 1740s. It is based mainly on the Newcastle Papers because Carteret left little personal correspondence. Pemberton is politically naive and very anti-Newcastle but does convey Carteret's wit, personal charm, and erudition, which made him such a contrast to the Duke.

345. Kemp, Betty. "Frederick, Prince of Wales" in Alex Natan, ed., *Silver Renaissance*, pp. 38-56. London: Macmillan, 1961.

A favorable biographical essay on the prince whose goals usually ran counter to the Pelhams'. In explaining Frederick's personal interests and political aims, Kemp does much to dispel the image of "Poor Fred" but does not identify the cause of his parents' dislike of him.

346. Gerrard, Christine. *The Patriot Opposition to Walpole: Politics, Poetry, and National Myth, 1725-1742*. Oxford: Clarendon Press, 1994.

This study examines how poetry and other forms of literature were used to promote the political views of the Patriot factions, especially the Cobham group.

It provides insight into the milieu in which the Pelhams had to work when they formed their administration in 1744.

347.   Owen, John B. *The Rise of the Pelhams*. London: Methuen, 1957.

The first modern study of the Pelhams' accession to power, in particular of the crucial period 1742-1743. Owen analyzes the composition of Commons to find the basis of the Pelhams' political strength and the platform on which they built their Broad-Bottom Administration. See also Harris (348).

348.   Harris, R., ed. "A Leicester House Political Diary, 1742-3" in *Camden Miscellany XXXI*, pp. 373-411. London: Royal Historical Society, 1992.

Not available to Owen (347), this diary kept by an agent of Frederick, Prince of Wales, gives details of the Pelhams' overtures to the Cobham faction, made while they were forming their administration.

349.   Ayling, Stanley. *The Elder Pitt, Earl of Chatham*. London: Collins, 1976.

The best modern biography of that enigmatic and charismatic politician but still not sufficiently detailed to do justice to its subject. The Pelhams put much time and thought into finding a way to silence or co-opt Pitt.

350.   Black, Jeremy. *Pitt the Elder*. Cambridge: Cambridge University Press, 1992.

This brief life incorporates revisions in assumptions about Pitt's abilities and leadership based on recent research.

351.   *Journal of the House of Commons* and *Journal of the House of Lords*. London: various dates.

The official records of proceedings in Parliament, including bills, resolutions, petitions, and papers. Pelham's actions and committee appointments can be followed in v.18-26 of the *Commons Journal*, and Newcastle's, in v.20-31 of the *Lords Journal*. Available on microfilm from the Center for Research Libraries, Chicago.

352.   Winstanley, D. A. *The University of Cambridge in the Eighteenth Century*. Cambridge: Cambridge University Press, 1922.

Newcastle was elected Chancellor of Cambridge in 1749. This book is chiefly "an account of Newcastle's activities as Chancellor", which Winstanley thought made the connection between the academic and political worlds too close for the University's good. The frontispiece is a portrait of the Duke which hangs in Clare Hall, his alma mater.

D. PELHAM AS CHIEF MINISTER

Pelham wore at least three hats. As First Lord of the Treasury, he was nominally head of the ministry, with as much power of decision as the King allowed him. As Chancellor of the Exchequer, he presented the budget to Commons and shepherded it through to approval. As Leader of Commons, he orchestrated the safe passage of bills promoted by the ministry and represented Commons to the King. He also wielded whatever influence the ministry and Crown could exert in elections.

353. Sedgwick, Romney. "Hon. Henry Pelham" in Sedgwick, *The History of Parliament: The House of Commons 1715-1754*, v.2, pp. 329-331. New York: Oxford University Press, 1970.

The entry is a synopsis of Pelham's career in Commons. The introductory survey (v.1) gives some details of his role as Leader of Commons and as manager of elections and of the legislation he guided.

354. Connors, Richard. "Pelham, Parliament and Public Policy, 1746-1754." Ph.D. thesis, Cambridge University, 1993.

This examination of how "Pelham's exercise of power and promotion of legislation contributed to the maintenance of political stability" considers two factors: political and parliamentary intrigue and social welfare legislation. Connors argues that the latter has been ignored in political studies, even though redress of grievances contributed greatly to public safety and tranquility.

355. Connors, Richard. "'The Grand Inquest of the Nation': Parliamentary Committees and Social Policy in Mid-Eighteenth-Century England." *Parliamentary History* 14 (1995): 285-313.

A study, based on (354), of specific pieces of legislation passed under Pelham's direction.

356. Connors, Richard. *The Politics of War and Peace in Mid-Eighteenth-Century England*. London: Macmillan, in press.

An expansion of the section on political and parliamentary intrigue in the author's dissertation (354) on Pelham as the Leader of Commons.

357.   Connors, Richard. *The Growth of Welfare in Hanoverian England 1733-1783*. London: Macmillan, forthcoming.

A revision of the section on social welfare legislation guided by Pelham, taken from the author's dissertation (354).

358.   Luff, P. A. "The Noblemen's Regiments: Politics and the 'Forty-Five." *Historical Research* 65 (1992): 54-73.

A good analysis of Pelham's political position. The Old Corps Whigs considered dangerous a plan to raise regiments financed by peers. Pelham had to balance their concerns against the ambitions of Bedford and other New Allies. The success of the regiments in the war silenced opposition and helped Pelham create a broad-based coalition.

359.   Luff, P. A. "Mathews *v.* Lestock: Parliament, Politics and the Navy in Mid-Eighteenth-Century England." *Parliamentary History* 10 (1991): 45-62.

This study of a Commons inquiry in 1745 into a failed naval engagement describes Pelham's attempt to manage debate on a divisive issue.

360.   Thomas, P.D.G. *The House of Commons in the Eighteenth Century*. Oxford: Clarendon Press, 1971.

Commons in the Pelham era was quite different from the modern House, especially in its membership and their relation to the ministry. Thomas explains the structure and functioning of that body and includes many references to both brothers.

361.   Sainty, J. C. "The Origin of the Leadership of the House of Lords." *Bulletin of the Institute of Historical Research* 47 (1974): 53-73.

An explanation of the role of the Leader of each House. Sainty shows that Newcastle led the House of Lords 1748-1762 (except for a nine-month break 1756-1757) and that Pelham assumed the lead in Commons while still Paymaster.

362.   Foord, Archibald. *His Majesty's Opposition 1714-1830*. Oxford: Clarendon Press, 1964.

The Pelhams faced opposition during both their rise to power and their administrations. Foord examines the controversies and chief participants in a parliamentary context.

363. Ilchester, Earl of. *Henry Fox, First Lord Holland.* New York: Scribner's, 1920. 2 vols.

Fox's prominence rests more on his competition with Pitt than on any actual accomplishments, although Pelham did use him as a deputy in Commons. This life was written by a family member and is out of date on politics but does give a good picture of the private man. The entries in the *History of Parliament* volumes are the only recent analysis of Fox's political career other than Luff (364).

364. Luff, P. A. "Henry Fox, the Duke of Cumberland and Pelhamite Politics, 1748-1757." Ph.D. thesis, Oxford University, 1981.

365. Whitworth, Rex. *William Augustus Duke of Cumberland: A Life.* London: Leo Cooper, 1992.

A military historian attempts to prove that the Duke's character and abilities have been maligned. The Pelhams' relations with Cumberland fluctuated, but he worked closely with Newcastle in the 1760s.

366. Fritz, Paul. *The English Ministers and Jacobitism between the Rebellions of 1715 and 1745.* Toronto: University of Toronto Press, 1975.

Essential background on Jacobite activities and how they influenced both the Pelhams' attitude toward this problem and the brothers' reaction to the 1745 Rebellion.

367. Haydon, Colin. *Anti-Catholicism in Eighteenth-Century England, c. 1714-80: A Political and Social Study.* Manchester: Manchester University Press, 1993.

"No Popery" was as much a political as a religious statement in Britain, particularly in the rebellion years of 1715 and 1745, for a Jacobite victory could replace a Hanoverian king with a Stuart and the Church of England with that of Rome. The Pelham ministry had to deal with public fears about the religious as well as the military aspect of the 1745 uprising. This study provides insight into the history and the depth of anti-Catholic sentiment.

368. Bricke, Margaret. "The Pelhams vs. Argyll: A Struggle for Mastery of

Scotland, 1747-1748." *Scottish Historical Review* 61 (1982): 157-165.

An examination of the Pelhams' effort to recover management of patronage in Scotland from the Duke of Argyll and the compromise effected after the crushing of the Jacobite Rebellion.

369. Beatty, J. L. "Henry Pelham and the Execution of Archibald Cameron." *Scottish Historical Review* 41 (1962): 46-50.

Beatty analyzes various theories of why Pelham waited until 1753 to obtain Cameron's execution for his part in 1745 Rebellion and concludes Pelham was masking the 1752 Elibank Plot, in which Cameron took part. Beatty suggests Pelham was protecting his conversion of the national debt from the financial panic that would surely result if the full extent of the Plot were revealed.

370. Cleary, Thomas. *Henry Fielding, Political Writer*. Waterloo: Wilfrid Laurier University Press, 1984.

Cleary traces Fielding's career and his political attachment to the Cobham faction, especially George Lyttelton. His friends' part in the Broad-Bottom Administration led Fielding to become a supporter of Pelham in his writings.

371. Battestin, Martin, with Ruth Battestin. *Henry Fielding: A Life*. London: Routledge, 1989.

This thoroughly documented work covers Fielding's relations with Pelham and Newcastle in great detail and is especially useful on his work as a London magistrate.

372. Black, Jeremy. "George II and the Juries Act: Royal Concern about the Control of the Press." *Historical Research* 61 (1988): 359-362.

The King was angry when a publisher of seditious pamphlets was acquitted in 1752 and complained to the Pelhams about the operation of the Juries Act of 1730. Black explains why the brothers did not think it politic to try to enact further control of the press.

373. Poole, Robert. "'Give Us Our Eleven Days!': Calendar Reform in Eighteenth-Century England." *Past & Present* 149 (1995): 93-139.

The 1752 bill to switch Britain from the Julian to the Gregorian calendar was one of the three bills most hotly debated in Pelham's last years in office. Poole examines the historical background and practical reasons for reform, the circumstances and content of the bill, public reaction to passage of the Act, and implementation of the new calendar. The extensive footnotes provide many sources concerning ideas about time and popular culture for the period.

374. Lemmings, David. "Marriage and the Law in the Eighteenth Century: Hardwicke's Marriage Act of 1753." *Historical Journal* 39 (1996): 339-360.

This second of the controversial bills that created management problems for the Pelhams was drafted by their good friend to prevent underage elopements. Lemmings analyzes the parliamentary debate on the bill, explains the background to and content of the Act, and examines the motives of its supporters and opponents.

375. Perry, Thomas. *Public Opinion, Propaganda, and Politics in Eighteenth-Century England: A Study of the Jew Bill of 1753*. Cambridge: Harvard University Press, 1962.

The Jewish Naturalization Act of 1753 was a rare and highly controversial political misjudgment by the Pelhams which they feared could threaten their success in the 1754 election. Perry examines the anti-Semitic publications used to whip up fierce public reaction.

376. Cranfield, G. A. "The *London Evening-Post* and the Jew Bill of 1753." *Historical Journal* 8 (1965): 16-30.

This article prints examples of the bitter attacks on the Pelhams published in this opposition newspaper because of the passage of the Bill. The force of misled public opinion convinced the Pelhams to seek repeal of the Act.

377. Harris, Rob. "The *London Evening Post* and Mid-Eighteenth-Century British Politics." *English Historical Review* 110 (1995): 1132-1156.

This more recent examination of the paper's influence goes beyond the question of the Jewish Naturalization Act, explaining the paper's Patriot editorial stance on a number of issues of the period.

378. Dickson, P.G.M. *The Financial Revolution in England: A Study in the Development of Public Credit 1688-1756*. London: Macmillan, 1967.

The seminal work on this complex topic. Dickson explains the founding of the public debt, the creation of the Sinking Fund, the South Sea Bubble and the financial reconstruction following its collapse, and the finances of war in the 1740s. Dickson provides the necessary context for the brothers' service at the Treasury and includes a favorable analysis of Pelham's career.

379.   Brewer, John. "The English State and Fiscal Appropriation, 1688-1789." *Politics & Society* 16 (1988): 335-385.

An analysis of the system that had been constructed for collection of taxes and what those taxes produced in this period. Brewer demonstrates how the system underpinned the structure of the British public debt. Useful in understanding the Pelhams' work at the Treasury.

380.   Brewer, John. *The Sinews of Power: War, Money, and the English State, 1688-1783*. New York: Knopf, 1989.

Brewer calls this a study of how and why Britain became a "fiscal-military state" in the eighteenth century. He looks at the growth of central government in response to the need to collect taxes, wage war, and foster international trade. While the work is not divided into specific periods, Brewer does give examples of how Pelham dealt with a number of problems. This volume makes clear the importance and power of the British government and, by implication, the great responsibility held by the Pelhams.

381.   Stone, Lawrence, ed. *An Imperial State at War: Britain from 1689 to 1815*. London: Routledge, 1994.

A volume of essays written in response to the ideas expounded by Brewer in (380). In his introduction, Stone sets out the importance of the concept of the fiscal-military state in a re-evaluation of the historiographical interpretation of eighteenth-century Britain. Of the contributors, Brewer writes on the theory of the state, E. A. Wrigley on society and the economy, Joanna Innes on how British involvement in frequent wars affected domestic society, Kathleen Wilson on how imperialism was reflected in domestic culture, Daniel Baugh on naval power and Atlantic trade, John Robertson on the evolution of the state after Union with Scotland in 1707, Ned Landsman on the role of Scotland and the American colonies in the empire, and Nicholas Canny on Ireland in the empire.

382.   Clark, Dora Mae. *The Rise of the British Treasury: Colonial Administration in the Eighteenth Century*. New Haven: Yale University Press, 1960.

A section on the Treasury under the Pelhams explains how they dealt with colonial finance and pressures from American trading interests.

383. Roseveare, Henry. *The Treasury: The Evolution of a British Institution.* London: Allan Lane, 1969.

A section on the eighteenth century examines the Treasury as the administrative center of government and provides anecdotal examples illustrating its structure and functions.

384. Sainty, J. C. *Office-Holders in Modern Britain: I. Treasury Officials 1660-1870.* London: Athlone Press, 1972.

This compendium of appointees includes notes on the composition of the administrative staff and on the powers, duties, and salaries of the offices held by the Pelhams.

385. Sutherland, Lucy. "Samson Gideon and the Reduction of Interest, 1749-50." *Economic History Review* 16 (1946): 15-29.

Gideon was an advisor to the Pelhams and one of the influential London financiers who brokered the annual public stock offering. Sutherland explains Pelham's plan to reduce interest on the National Debt during peacetime, an important measure that strengthened the economy and the nation.

386. Hoppit, Julian. *Risk and Failure in English Business 1700-1800.* Cambridge: Cambridge University Press, 1987.

This study of bankruptcy provides insight into the business climate and includes data on economic cycles, weather fluctuations, and harvest yields and prices in Pelham era.

387. Rogers, Nicholas. *Whigs and Cities: Popular Politics in the Age of Walpole and Pitt.* Oxford: Clarendon Press, 1989.

No ministry could ignore the great political and economic power of London, wielded primarily through its Common Council. Rogers points out how the Pelhams were influenced on questions of money-raising and foreign policy.

388. Namier, Sir Lewis. "The Cabinet" in his *Crossroads of Power*, pp. 93-110. London: Hamilton, 1962.

Namier explains the many differences between modern and eighteenth-century cabinets and reviews, mostly unfavorably, what other historians have written about the latter. He also analyzes the composition of the Cabinet during both the Pelham brothers' administrations.

389. Sedgwick, Romney. "The Inner Cabinet from 1739-41." *English Historical Review* 34 (1919): 290-302.

Sedgwick demonstrates that the Pelhams were members of the inner or efficient Cabinet for several years before Walpole's fall and that Newcastle often drew up the formal statements of the collective decisions.

390. Reitan, E. A. "The Civil List in Eighteenth-Century British Politics: Parliamentary Supremacy Versus the Independence of the Crown." *Historical Journal* 3 (1966): 318-337.

The reduction of the charge on the Civil List effected by Henry Pelham won him George II's gratitude. By law, the monarch received annual revenue to pay all expenses of running the government except those of the national debt and the armed forces. If revenue exceeded these expenses, called the Civil List, the King kept the surplus. Parliament's obligation to make up shortfalls in that revenue provided opportunities for opponents to question the ministry's use of the revenue, as the Pelhams well knew.

E. NEWCASTLE AS SECRETARY OF STATE

In 1724, the Duke was appointed Secretary of State for the Southern Department, responsible for France, Switzerland, Italy, Spain, Portugal, Turkey, the Channel Islands, the British colonies, and Ireland, together with a share of domestic affairs. In 1748 he moved to the Northern Department, which handled relations with the German states, Austria, Prussia, Holland, Scandinavia, Poland, and Russia. The Northern Secretary also was responsible for a share of domestic affairs.

391. Thomson, M. A. *The Secretaries of State 1681-1782*. Oxford: Clarendon Press, 1932.

Still the standard work on the function and powers of the office, despite its age. Thomson draws many of his illustrations from Newcastle's private and official correspondence. Sections are devoted to various responsibilities: Scotland, Ireland, and the colonies; the Army and Navy; foreign affairs; domestic affairs; the Secret Service and the *London Gazette*.

392. Sainty, J. C. *Office-Holders in Modern Britain: II. Officials of the Secretaries of State 1660-1782*. London: Athlone, Press, 1973.

The valuable introduction explains the organization of the secretariat and its division into Northern and Southern Departments. Sainty lists the duties and salaries of each office in the secretariat. In addition to providing details about Newcastle's official position, this work clarifies the status of a number of his correspondents.

393. Ellis, Kenneth. *The Post Office in the Eighteenth Century: A Study in Administrative History*. London: Oxford University Press, 1958.

For the Secretaries of State, the post office circulated printed propaganda within Britain, intercepted and deciphered diplomatic mail, and gathered intelligence from a network of domestic and foreign agents. Ellis comments on the Pelhams' relations with the postal staff.

394. Williams, Basil. *Carteret and Newcastle: A Contrast in Contemporaries*. Cambridge: Cambridge University Press, 1943. Reprinted by Archon Books in 1966.

Compared to Newcastle, Carteret had a far more pleasing personality. He was a witty, erudite polyglot who shone in company, notwithstanding his tendency to overindulge in wine. Here, Williams contrasts Carteret's concentration on foreign policy with what Williams calls Newcastle's "career of electioneer-in-chief" of the Whigs. Williams' contempt for Newcastle's foibles blinds him to the Duke's real strengths as a politician and minister. Brief family histories and genealogical tables are included in this work.

395. Horn, D. B. *Great Britain and Europe in the Eighteenth Century*. Oxford: Clarendon Press, 1967.

This work has been superseded by more recent studies but still is a useful introduction to the subject of foreign affairs because it covers British relations with individual countries in separate sections, each with its own bibliography. Newcastle of course figures prominently throughout this work.

396. Black, Jeremy. "Britain's Foreign Alliances in the Eighteenth Century." *Albion* 20 (1988): 573-602.

Prof. Black has replaced Sir Richard Lodge as the leading writer on foreign policy in the Pelham era. The bibliographies in his works are especially useful for finding sources on particular aspects of foreign affairs. Here he assesses how the British political system and the constraints of domestic pressure affected ministers' ability to negotiate alliances.

397.   Black, Jeremy. *A System of Ambition? British Foreign Policy 1660-1793*. London: Longman, 1991.

This overview summarizes Black's ideas and provides the background and context of Newcastle's actions.

398.   Black, Jeremy. *British Foreign Policy in the Age of Walpole*. Edinburgh: Donald, 1985.

An analysis of what factors influenced formulation of policy while Newcastle was Southern Secretary.

399.   Black, Jeremy. "The British Navy and British Foreign Policy in the First Half of the Eighteenth Century" in Karl Schweizer and Black, eds., *Essays in European History in Honour of Ragnhild Hatton*, pp. 137-155. Lennoxville: Bishop's University, 1985.

A useful short examination of the relationship between naval power and foreign policy goals based on opinions of diplomats and admirals. Black points out the limitations of the British navy in the 1720s and 1730s. A quotation from a 1737 Pelham speech on the interdependence of the Army and Navy is included.

400.   Black, Jeremy. *Natural and Necessary Enemies: Anglo-French Relations in the Eighteenth Century*. London: Duckworth, 1986.

This study of relations 1713-1793 explains the points of conflict and the reasons why Newcastle saw France as the chief threat to Britain's security.

401.   Black, Jeremy. *The Collapse of the Anglo-French Alliance 1727-1731*. New York: St. Martin's Press, 1987.

This detailed examination of the breakdown in relations after the accession of George II includes an account of Newcastle's role in the policy dispute between Walpole and Townshend.

402.   Wilson, A. M. *French Foreign Policy During the Administration of Cardinal Fleury, 1726-43*. Cambridge: Harvard University Press, 1936.

Despite its age, this work is still a useful account of the conduct of France's foreign relations by her most able minister. Like most historians in the 1930s, Wilson misjudges Newcastle.

403. Black, Jeremy. "The Development of Anglo-Sardinian Relations in the First Half of the Eighteenth Century." *Studi piemontesi* 12 (1983): 48-60.

The Italian states fell within Newcastle's province as Southern Secretary. Black explains how British relations with Sardinia fluctuated in a way that reflected changes in British relations with France.

404. Dunthorne, Hugh. *The Maritime Powers 1721-1740: A Study of Anglo-Dutch Relations in the Age of Walpole.* New York: Garland, 1986.

A detailed study of the political relations between the two allies up to the War of the Austrian Succession and how their interests came to diverge. Valuable for understanding the Pelhams' policies after 1743.

405. Dunthorne, Hugh. "Prince and Republic: The House of Orange in Dutch and Anglo-Dutch Politics During the First Half of the Eighteenth Century" in Karl Schweizer and Jeremy Black, eds., *Essays in European History in Honour of Ragnhild Hatton*, pp. 19-34. Lennoxville: Bishop's University, 1985.

The marriage of George II's daughter Anna to William of Orange in 1734 only further complicated the difficulties the British Secretaries of State encountered in dealing with the Dutch.

406. Sperling, John G. *The South Sea Company: An Historical Essay and Bibliographical Finding List.* Boston: Harvard Graduate School of Business Administration, 1962.

The activities and demands of the Company frequently disrupted the plans of the Southern Secretary for dealing with Spain. This brief history of the company clarifies its position in the negotiations for the Treaty of Seville (1729) and in the war of 1739.

407. Lodge, Richard. "The Treaty of Seville (1729)." *Transactions of the Royal Historical Society* 4th ser. 16 (1933): 1-42.

Lodge contends that Fleury used the Treaty to involve Britain (and Newcastle) in circumstances leading to a future war.

408.   Cady, Priscilla. "Horatio Walpole and the Making of the Treaty of Seville, 1728-1730." Ph.D. thesis, Ohio State University, 1976.

This study accepts Walpole's claims in his *Apology* and credits the Treaty's enactment to him. Cady says Walpole was involved in the writing of the provisional treaty and its rewriting to meet Spanish objections and that he personally persuaded Cardinal Fleury to accept the changes. Walpole had everything in order by the time Stanhope arrived, so that the Secretary had only to sign the Treaty in November 1729. Walpole then returned to London and persuaded Parliament to approve the Treaty.

409.   Black, Jeremy. "British Neutrality in the War of the Polish Succession, 1733-1735." *International History Review* 8 (1986): 345-366.

Black offers a reinterpretation of George II's complex attitudes toward this conflict and points out how the difficult relations between Hanover and Prussia prevented the formation of a true Anglo-Austrian alliance in 1731-1733. He contends the King's influence was decisive on the question of British neutrality and was based on his distrust of Austrian policy in the Empire.

410.   Lodge, Richard. "English Neutrality in the War of Polish Succession." *Transactions of the Royal Historical Society* 4th ser. 14 (1931): 141-173.

Lodge gives a history of the negotiations undertaken prior to the war, describes the effect of Horace Walpole's relations with Fleury on Sir Robert's policy, and offers reasons why Newcastle was right in opposing neutrality.

411.   Black, Jeremy. "Mid-Eighteenth Century Conflict with Particular Reference to the Wars of the Polish and Austrian Successions" in Black, ed., *The Origins of War in Early Modern Europe*, pp. 210-241. Edinburgh: John Donald, 1987.

An examination of how the dynastic interests of individual monarchs affected state policy and influenced the outbreak or avoidance of war. Black suggests less emphasis be placed on the modern historiographical search for impersonal trends and more room given to the unpredictability of international relations and to eighteenth-century opinion on the causes of war.

412.   Woodfine, Philip, ed. "Horace Walpole and British Relations with Spain, 1738" in *Camden Miscellany XXXII*, pp. 289-328. London: Royal Historical Society, 1994.

Walpole felt his experience as a diplomat qualified him to draw up this assessment of the state of relations for his brother Sir Robert and the Cabinet at a time when the ministry was under great pressure from London merchants and the Patriot faction to take action against Spain. Woodfine's introduction explains the context and Newcastle's difficult position as Southern Secretary.

413.   Woodfine, Philip. "Ideas of Naval Power and the Conflict with Spain, 1737-1742" in Jeremy Black and Woodfine, eds., *The British Navy and the Use of Naval Power in the Eighteenth Century*, pp. 71-90. Atlantic Highlands, NJ: Humanities Press, 1989.

Public demand for war against Spain was based on delusions of British naval supremacy. When the war went badly, the public blamed Walpole. Woodfine explains the true weaknesses of naval operations, the divisions within the ministry, and the role of the "crucial figure" in the mounting of the West Indies expedition, Newcastle.

414.   Harding, Richard. "Sir Robert Walpole's Ministry and the Conduct of the War with Spain, 1739-41." *Historical Research* 60 (1987): 299-320.

A naval historian, Harding defends the ministry against charges of mismanaging the war, citing the difficulties inherent in trying to move the country quickly out of a peace status to meet the "unprecedented demands" of trans-Atlantic war. An important factor was the time needed to gather men and supplies to bring the Navy up to war footing. Harding offers a favorable analysis of Newcastle's plans and actions.

415.   Woodfine, Philip. "The Anglo-Spanish War of 1739" in Jeremy Black, ed., *The Origins of War in Early Modern Europe*, pp. 185-209. Edinburgh: John Donald, 1987.

While admitting British domestic politics to be an important factor in the outbreak of the war, Woodfine points out how Spanish policy and the instability of its royal family contributed. He also explains the complicated trade relations between the two nations and deflates the episode of Jenkins' ear, attributing the war to the inability of the two sides to compromise their differences. Newcastle shows well in this assessment.

416.   Black, Jeremy. "Parliament and Foreign Policy 1739-1763." *Parliaments, Estates and Representation* 12 (1992): 121-142.

In this assessment of Parliament's influence on foreign policy, Black examines debate on the major issues of the period, quoting several speeches by Pelham.

No scholarly biography of George II has been published, possibly because he left so few personal papers. The following works about him and his beloved Hanover together provide a portrait of him and make it clear that, despite his grandson's misconceptions, George was never the prisoner of his ministers.

417.   Newman, Aubrey. *The World Turned Inside Out: New Views on George II.* Leicester: Leicester University Reprographic Unit, 1988.

Gaining and keeping the King's favor was crucial to the Pelhams' hold on office. This study dispels the notion of an inactive monarch and shows George II as a full participant in the governing of Britain. Newman also explains the conflict created by George's being both King of Great Britain and Elector of Hanover.

418.   Owen, J. B. "George II Reconsidered" in Anne Whiteman, J. S. Bromley, and P.G.M. Dickson, eds., *Statesmen, Scholars and Merchants*, pp. 113-134. Oxford: Clarendon Press, 1973.

Owen assesses the King's temperament, his attitude on particular issues, and his relations with the Pelhams and concludes George was the "dominant voice in the conduct of war and diplomacy."

419.   Black, Jeremy. "George II Reconsidered: A Consideration of George's Influence in the Conduct of Foreign Policy, in the First Years of His Reign." *Mitteilungen des Österreichischen Staatsarchiv* 35 (1982): 35-56.

Black asserts that the King was able to dictate foreign policy in the area that most concerned him, Baltic and German affairs, and was well aware of the need to gain Parliament's support for his policies. He also examines the King's relations with his Secretaries of State.

420.   Brauer, Gert. *Die hannoversch-englischen Subsidienverträge 1702-1748.* Aslen: Scientia Verlag, 1962.

This study examines the connection between the role of the British king as Elector of Hanover and British employment of Hanoverian troops in time of war, a controversial issue in Commons. Brauer utilizes material from the Hanoverian archives and includes many quotations in English from parliamentary debate on the question.

421.   Dann, Uriel. *Hanover and Great Britain 1740-1760: Diplomacy and Survival.* Leicester: Leicester University Press, 1991.

An analysis of the influence of George II's status as Elector of Hanover on British foreign policy and on the position of Hanover in continental politics. Dann gives special attention to Newcastle's good working relations with the Hanoverian Chancery.

422. Mediger, W. "Great Britain, Hanover and the Rise of Prussia" in Ragnhild Hatton and M. S. Anderson, eds., *Studies in Diplomatic History*, pp. 199-233. London: Archon, 1970.

Mediger explains the awkward relations between the two German states and Newcastle's cooperation with the Hanoverian Chancellor Baron von Münchhausen.

423. Schlenke, Manfred. *England und das Friderizianische Preussen 1740-1763*. Munich: Alber, 1963.

This detailed study of relations between the two powers in the course of two wars includes much about the Pelhams. A list of pertinent pamphlets is appended. Schweizer's work on the Seven Year War has superseded the latter part of Schlenke's study.

424. Baugh, D. A. "Great Britain's 'Blue-Water' Policy, 1689-1815." *International History Review* 10 (1988): 33-58.

After 1700, many Englishmen began to believe naval power was the best guard of international trade and of their country in war. Others believed rising French military power had to be combatted on land. These two opinions influenced how Secretaries shaped British foreign policy. This article provides background and examples of the Pelhams' policy.

425. Baugh, Daniel. *British Naval Administration in the Age of Walpole*. Princeton: Princeton University Press, 1965.

This study of administrative problems comments on the Admiralty's relations with Pelham at the Treasury and Newcastle as Secretary of State.

426. Black, Jeremy. "Naval Power and British Foreign Policy in the Age of Pitt the Elder" in Black and Philip Woodfine, eds., *The British Navy and the Use of Naval Power in the Eighteenth Century*, pp. 91-107. Atlantic Highlands, NJ: Humanities Press, 1989.

Black's analysis of the period 1740-1760 indicates that British naval power allayed fear of invasion but was of little use as a bargaining chip in foreign policy negotiations for alliances.

427. Conn, Stetson. *Gibraltar in British Diplomacy in the Eighteenth Century.* New Haven: Yale University Press, 1942.

A history of British control of the Mediterranean stronghold and its position in British-Spanish relations. Newcastle usually opposed any ceding or exchange of Gibraltar for other territory.

428. Scott, H. M. " 'The True Principles of the Revolution': The Duke of Newcastle and the Idea of the Old System" in Jeremy Black, ed., *Knights Errant and True Englishmen: British Foreign Policy, 1660-1800,* pp. 55-91. Edinburgh: Donald, 1989.

An important analysis of the assumptions underlying foreign policy and the significance of the language employed. The Old System of alliance with Austria and the Dutch was devised by William III to stymie France and, despite its weaknesses and failures, was adopted by Newcastle in 1744 because it embodied Whig ideas about how diplomacy should be conducted.

429. Horn, D. B. "The Duke of Newcastle and the Origins of the Diplomatic Revolution" in J. H. Elliott and H. G. Koenigsberger, *The Diversity of History,* pp. 247-268. Ithaca: Cornell University Press, 1970.

In this dated but still useful study, Horn asserts that Newcastle gradually adopted Carteret's foreign policy and was able, with Hardwicke's help, to overcome Pelham's "misguided" objections to this course of action. Horn says that the Duke, while trying to regain former allies after 1748, misunderstood Austria's needs and intentions and inadvertently pushed her toward alliance with France. See Browning (431-432) for a different opinion.

430. Horn, D. B. "The Cabinet Controversy on Subsidy Treaties in Time of Peace, 1749-50." English Historical Review 45 (1930): 463-466.

Newcastle believed subsidies were necessary to outbid France for allies, despite Pelham's desire to retrench during peacetime. Horn explains how the Duke overcame his brother's objections to some of these foreign grants.

431. Browning, Reed. "The Duke of Newcastle and the Imperial Election Plan, 1749-1754." Journal of British Studies 7 (1967): 28-47.

Browning defends Newcastle's ability as Secretary of State, the quality of his plan, and his negotiations on the question of who should become the next emperor of the Holy Roman Empire.

432. Browning, Reed. "The British Orientation of Austrian Foreign Policy, 1749-1754." *Central European History* 1 (1968): 299-323.

In this article, Browning contends that Austria, despite Kaunitz, worked to maintain its ties with Britain even while resisting Newcastle's Imperial Election Plan.

F. NEWCASTLE AT THE TREASURY

While the Duke was able to succeed his brother as First Lord of the Treasury and nominal leader of the ministry, he could not assume his roles in Commons. Building a reliable working relationship with Commoners capable of filling those roles, yet willing to forego Pelham's power, proved difficult. This instability, combined with the demands war made upon the ministry, left Newcastle's administration less united than his brother's had been.

433. Clark, J.C.D. *The Dynamics of Change: The Crisis of the 1750s and English Party Systems.* Cambridge: Cambridge University Press, 1982.

A thorough and detailed examination of Newcastle's political activities from the death of Pelham to the Duke's 1757 coalition with Pitt, the best available even though the narrative is sometimes obscured by the plethora of facts and the author's political theories. Clark contends that Newcastle always controlled the political situation and was not forced by public opinion to ally with Pitt. See Peters (437) for a different opinion.

434. Namier, Sir Lewis, and John Brooke. *The History of Parliament: The House of Commons 1754-1790.* London: HMSO, 1964. 3 vols.

The introduction (v.1) provides information on activities in Commons during Newcastle's administration. Entries (v.2-3) for leading politicians like Pitt and Fox contribute to an understanding of Newcastle's problems in dealing with Commons and add details of how they treated the Duke's financial measures.

435. Kulisheck, P. J. "The Favourite Child of the Whigs: The Life and Career of Henry Bilson Legge, 1708-1764." Ph.D. thesis, University of Minnesota, 1996.

This study of Newcastle's Chancellor of the Exchequer explains the Duke's often-difficult relations with both Legge and Pitt, the reasons why the latter two fell out over what policy to pursue, and how Bute's interference in the Hampshire election allowed Newcastle to recover his influence with Legge.

436.   Luff, P. A. "Henry Fox and the 'Lead' in the House of Commons 1754-1755." *Parliamentary History* 6 (1987): 33-46.

Fox expected to succeed Pelham as Leader of Commons but failed to negotiate an understanding with Newcastle. His resulting distrust of the Duke and his subsequent conflicts with Pitt made Fox resentful.

437.   Peters, Marie. *Pitt and Popularity: The Patriot Minister and London Opinion during the Seven Years' War*. Oxford: Clarendon Press, 1980.

This study of Pitt's manipulation of public opinion explains the issues that most excited dispute and how the nominally Tory newspaper the *Monitor* supported Pitt. Peters also clarifies Newcastle's position within the coalition. See Clark (433) for a different opinion.

438.   Newman, A. N., ed. "Leicester House Politics, 1750-60" in *Camden Miscellany XXIII*, pp. 85-228. London: Royal Historical Society, 1969.

Extracts taken from the papers of the 2nd Earl of Egmont illustrate the intentions of Frederick, Prince of Wales, for his reign, the consequences of his death in 1751, and how his followers (Leicester House) interacted with the Pelhams while regrouping around Prince George.

439.   McKelvey, James. *George III and Lord Bute: The Leicester House Years*. Durham: Duke University Press, 1973.

A sometimes erroneous study of the attempt by Prince George and his advisor Bute to influence a 1759 by- election and to undermine Newcastle's position by building their own patronage network.

440.   Elliot, G.F.S. *The Border Elliots and the Family of Minto*. Edinburgh: Douglas, 1897.

Gilbert Elliot, M.P., was a close associate of Bute. The many quotations from his correspondence in this volume contain information on Bute's relations with Newcastle.

441.   Wilson, Charles. *Anglo-Dutch Commerce & Finance in the Eighteenth Century*. Cambridge: Cambridge University Press, 1941, reprinted 1966.

Dutch investment in the British national debt was an important factor in the success of the Pelhams as First Lord of the Treasury. Each year when the Loan was opened to investors, many of the stockbrokers buying large blocks for resale were acting for Dutch clients. After an examination of trade as the source of Dutch wealth, Wilson explains the activities of these stockbrokers, whose names appear so frequently in Newcastle's correspondence.

442. Carter, Alice Clare. *Getting, Spending and Investing in Early Modern Times: Essays on Dutch, English and Huguenot Economic History*. Assen: Van Gorcum, 1975.

While all 12 essays throw light on eighteenth-century public finance, three apply particularly to the Pelhams. An explanation of the history and structure of the English public debt written especially for students clarifies the debt's place in political discussion. Examinations of the Dutch as neutrals in the Seven Years War and Anglo-Dutch trade disputes in 1759 draw upon the Hardwicke and Newcastle Papers. Also included are an article by Wilson (441) disputing Carter's conclusions about the size of Dutch investment in the British debt and Carter's rebuttal.

443. Bullion, John. "The *Monitor* and the Beer Tax Controversy: A Study of Constraints on London Newspapers of 1760-1761" in Karl Schweizer and Jeremy Black, eds., *Politics and the Press in Hanoverian Britain*, pp. 89-117. Lewiston: Mellen, 1989.

An analysis of the difficulties Newcastle and Legge encountered when they proposed an increase in the tax on strong beer and of press reaction to the proposal.

444. Lawson, Philip. *George Grenville: A Political Life*. Oxford: Clarendon Press, 1984.

Newcastle always feared Pitt would press him to make Grenville, whom the Duke strongly disliked, Chancellor of the Exchequer. Grenville was convinced of the superiority of his own talents and plans and, aligning himself with Bute, helped to drive Newcastle from office.

445. Schweizer, Karl, and John Bullion. "The Vote of Credit Controversy, 1762." *British Journal for Eighteenth-Century Studies* 15 (1992): 175-188.

A study of how the dispute over the state of public credit and the sum needed

to continue the war was used by Bute and Grenville as a lever to force
Newcastle's resignation.

G. NEWCASTLE'S LAST YEARS

The Duke's ministerial influence effectively died with his master George II in
October 1760, although some time passed before this became evident, even to
Newcastle. The new young King was determined to rule as he thought best and
through the men he chose. He would keep Newcastle in his service just as long
as that proved expedient.

446.   Namier, Sir Lewis. *The Structure of Politics at the Accession of George
           III*. London: Macmillan, 1965. 2nd ed.

This work, first published in 1929, laid the foundation for Namier's reputation
as an historian, which reached its peak in the 1950s. He used this study of
government and Parliament 1760-1762 under Newcastle and Bute to dispel the
notion of a two-party system, to show that the supposed corruption funded by
the Court was insignificant, and to assert that George III was not an unconstitu-
tional ruler.

447.   Namier, Sir Lewis. *England in the Age of the American Revolution*. New
           York: St. Martin's Press, 1961. 2nd ed.

Namier expanded on his refutation of traditional Whig theories in this work,
first published in 1931. This study of the membership, elections, and control of
the House of Commons has much to say about Newcastle's activities.

448.   Christie, Ian. "George III and the Historians--Thirty Years On." *History*
           71 (1986): 205-221.

After reviewing old estimates of George III and George II, Christie points out
how new evidence has caused historians to reassess the character and activities
of these kings.

449.   Brooke, John. *King George III*. London: Constable, 1972.

450.   Ayling, Stanley. *George the Third*. New York: Knopf, 1972.

Standard biographies, with differing strengths, of the King who reigned for 60
years. See Christie (448) for more recent opinions.

451.   Schweizer, Karl, ed. *Lord Bute: Essays in Re-interpretation*. Leicester:
           Leicester University Press, 1988.

All of the essays in this volume throw new light on the young King's "dear friend" and his relations with Newcastle. See especially Frank O'Gorman's "The Myth of Lord Bute's Secret Influence" (pp. 57-81), which examines the Newcastle Whigs' pet theory that Bute retained his hold on the King after leaving office.

452.   Schweizer, Karl. "Foreign Policy and the Eighteenth-Century English Press: The Case of Israel Mauduit's *Considerations on the Present German War." Publishing History* 39 (1996): 45-53.

Mauduit's pamphlet arguing against continuance of the war in Germany aroused wide-spread public discussion when it was published in 1760 and went through several editions. Schweizer looks at the printed replies it elicited and why the controversy made it difficult for Newcastle to secure renewal of the Prussian subsidy.

453.   Bullion, John, and Karl Schweizer. "The Use of the Private Papers of Politicians in the Study of Policy Formulation During the 18th Century: The Bute Papers as a Case Study." *Archives* 22 (1995): 34-44.

The authors explain how the works of early and modern diplomatic historians differ in approach and methodology and also throw light on the quarrel of Bute and Newcastle over supplies needed for the conduct of the war in 1762.

454.   O'Gorman, Frank. *The Rise of Party in England: The Rockingham Whigs 1760-82.* London: Allen & Unwin, 1975.

This work examines the formation of the new Whig Party around Newcastle and his young supporters and describes his last period in office as Lord Privy Seal.

455.   Langford, Paul. *The First Rockingham Administration 1765-1766.* London: Oxford University Press, 1973.

This study of the Whig ministry that repealed the Stamp Act clarifies Newcastle's role and the decline of his influence.

456.   McCahill, Michael. "The House of Lords in the 1760s" in Clyve Jones, ed., *A Pillar of the Constitution: The House of Lords in British Politics, 1640-1784,* pp. 165-198. London: Hambledon Press, 1989.

McCahill's account of the peers' reactions to the changes of the new reign is useful on Newcastle's last years in politics. McCahill also comments on the accuracy of the Duke's "Narrative". See Bateson (199).

457. Watson, D. H. "The Relations between the Duke of Newcastle, the Marquis of Rockingham and Mercantile Interests in London and the Provinces, 1761-68." Ph.D. thesis, Sheffield University, 1968.

9

Special Topics

A. NEWCASTLE'S ECCLESIASTICAL PATRONAGE

Because the British monarch is head of the Anglican Church, the Crown, in the eighteenth century, selected appointees to the hierarchy. In practice, ministers usually presented a list of candidates from which the King could make a choice or reject all. The Crown also had the right to present (recommend) clergy to some but not all livings (appointments for life as rector or vicar of a parish). Newcastle assumed management of this Crown patronage in 1736 and, as a genuinely devout man, tried to find properly qualified clergymen who were also reliable Whigs.

458. Taylor, S.J.C. "Church and State in England in the Mid-Eighteenth Century: The Newcastle Years, 1742-1762." Ph.D. thesis, Cambridge University, 1987.

Taylor contends that the Church was an integral part of politics but that its interests were not totally subordinated to those of the state. His thesis includes sections on the physical and spiritual state of the Church, the management of the Crown's ecclesiastical patronage, ministers' and clergy's perception of the Church's role, and conflicts between the Church and the state.

459. Taylor, Stephen. *Church and State Under the Whig Supremacy 1714-1760.* Cambridge University Press, forthcoming.

460. Taylor, Stephen. "The Bishops at Westminster in the Mid-Eighteenth Century" in Clyve Jones, ed., *A Pillar of the Constitution: The House of Lords in British Politics, 1640-1784*, pp. 137-164. London: Hambledon, 1989.

In this article, Taylor examines the bishops' voting record in the House of

Lords and the degree of their loyalty to Newcastle in divisions over controversial issues.

461. Taylor, Stephen. "'The Fac Totum in Ecclesiastical Affairs'?: The Duke of Newcastle and the Crown's Ecclesiastical Patronage." *Albion* 24 (1992): 409-433.

Here Taylor reassesses Newcastle's ability to control Crown patronage, the role of George II, and the balance of power within the ministry and concludes the Duke's control was "far less absolute" than previously believed.

462. Cross, Arthur. *The Anglican Episcopate and the American Colonies.* New York: Longmans, 1902.

This old but seminal study of clerical attitudes about the setting up of an episcopate in the colonies provides context for Newcastle's position on the question and prints portions of his correspondence.

463. Taylor, Stephen. "Whigs, Bishops and America: The Politics of Church Reform in Mid-Eighteenth Century England." *Historical Journal* 36 (1993): 331-356.

Newcastle believed that creating an Anglican episcopate in America would alienate the Dissenters, who usually supported the Whigs. The bishops agreed with the Pelhams that attempts at any clerical reform might renew national controversy over religion.

464. Olson, Alison G. "The Eighteenth Century Empire: The London Dissenters Lobbies and the American Colonies." *Journal of American Studies* 26 (1992): 41-58.

This article throws light on the controversy over a bishopric for the American Anglican Church and Pelham and Newcastle's dealings with colonial representatives.

465. Macauley, John S., and R. W. Greaves, eds. *The Autobiography of Thomas Secker, Archbishop of Canterbury.* Lawrence: University of Kansas Libraries, 1988.

A thoroughly annotated edition of the memoirs of a close associate of the Pelhams provides information on the Church, politics, and Newcastle's relations with the Anglican hierarchy.

466. Sykes, Norman. *Church and State in England in the Eighteenth Century.* Cambridge: Cambridge University Press, 1934.

Sykes explains the context of the Duke's activities and how his faith qualified him for the post. Sykes' work should be compared to Taylor's (458-459) because the latter had access to more sources.

467. Sykes, Norman. "The Duke of Newcastle as Ecclesiastical Minister." *English Historical Review* 57 (1942): 59-84.

An analysis of Newcastle's dealings with the clergy and with George II for securing approval of bishops' appointments, the Duke's loss of patronage under George III, and his effectiveness as ecclesiastical minister.

468. Barnes, Donald G. "The Duke of Newcastle, Ecclesiastical Minister, 1724-1754." *Pacific Historical Review* 3 (1934): 164-191.

Barnes covers much the same ground as Sykes (467) but doesn't analyze the quality of the appointments recommended by Newcastle. Barnes compares the styles of letters written by different types of applicants for patronage, such as peers and clergy.

469. Hirschberg, D. R. "The Government and Church Patronage in England, 1660-1760." *Journal of British Studies* 20 (1980): 109-139.

This study of which persons actually controlled appointments to livings includes a favorable assessment of Newcastle as the coordinator of Crown patronage.

470. Gibson, William. "Patterns of Nepotism and Kinship in the Eighteenth-Century Church." *Journal of Religious History* 14 (1987): 382-389.

This analysis includes information on Newcastle's relations with clergymen seeking Church appointments for their relatives.

471. Gibson, William. "'Importunate Cries of Misery': The Correspondence of Lucius Henry Hibbens and the Duke of Newcastle, 1741-58." *British Library Journal* 17 (1991): 87-93.

Hibbens' distinctive spiky handwriting quickly becomes familiar to researchers using the Newcastle Papers. Gibson uses his letters to illustrate the Duke's patronage relations with ordinary clergymen seeking preferment.

472. Bateson, Mary. "Clerical Preferment under the Duke of Newcastle." *English Historical Review* 7 (1892): 685-696.

This article includes quotations from letters about preferment written by clergymen but provides little analysis of Newcastle's activities.

B. THE PELHAMS AND AMERICA

A thorough, up-to-date study of the Pelhams' conduct of American affairs does not exist. Most of the works listed here are rather old and deal with Newcastle's activities as Secretary of State.

473.   Basye, Arthur. *The Lords Commissioners of Trade and Plantations Commonly Known as the Board of Trade.* New Haven: Yale University Press, 1925.

The Board struggled with successive Southern Secretaries over control of the colonies but was hindered by poor leadership until the appointment of the Earl of Halifax in 1748. Basye takes an unfavorable view of Newcastle's role.

474.   Henretta, James A. *"Salutary Neglect: Colonial Administration under the Duke of Newcastle."* Princeton, NJ: Princeton University Press, 1972.

In this study of Newcastle's management of the American colonies, Henretta faults the Duke for using patronage for British political ends and for not providing goals and guidance for colonial economic and political life. See Haffenden (475) for a different opinion.

475.   Haffenden, Philip. "Colonial Appointments and Patronage under the Duke of Newcastle, 1724-1739." *English Historical Review* 78 (1963): 417-435.

Haffenden defends Newcastle's work as colonial secretary, points out what he calls misjudgments of the Duke in earlier studies, and finds no damage resulting from Newcastle's use of patronage.

476.   Katz, Stanley N. *Newcastle's New York: Anglo-American Politics, 1732-1753.* Cambridge: Harvard University Press, 1968.

This author portrays Newcastle as the "perfect administrator" of a system chiefly concerned with the colonies' economic role in the empire. Katz says Newcastle "had no conception of colonial policy" and "viewed administration as a branch of politics," filling colonial offices to suit patronage needs in England.

477.   Buffington, A. H. "The Canadian Expedition of 1746: Its Relation to British Politics." *American Historical Review* 45 (1939-1940): 552-580.

According to Buffington, domestic politics induced the Pelhams to support this American venture. Naval operations were more popular in Commons than continental warfare, and the concession pleased their new allies Bedford and Pitt, who promoted the Expedition.

478. Clayton, T. R. "The Duke of Newcastle, the Earl of Halifax and the American Origins of the Seven Years' War." *Historical Journal* 24 (1981): 571-603.

Clayton contends that, after 1748, Newcastle knew of and was alarmed by French encroachment on the British American colonies but believed force should be used for protection only if a general war could be avoided. He says that misleading despatches from Europe and British hawks who discounted the possibility of a general war negated the Duke's position.

479. Temperley, H. W. "The Relations of England with Spanish America, 1720-44." *The Annual Report of the AHA 1911*, v.1, pp. 231-38.

A dated but interesting analysis of how policy was influenced, especially in 1739.

480. Manning, Frederick J. "The Duke of Newcastle and the West Indies: A Study of Colonial and Diplomatic Policies of the Secretary of State for the Southern Department, 1713-1754." Ph.D. thesis, Yale University, 1926.

A favorable assessment of Newcastle's work which does not clearly prove its argument. Manning says the Duke was "constantly open to new ideas", learned from his mistakes in the West Indies in the 1740s, and as a result completely reversed his diplomatic and colonial policies. He contends that Newcastle's early measures to pressure Spain and his strategy during the war were all subverted by colonial merchants and planters.

C. THE WAR OF THE AUSTRIAN SUCCESSION

Historians use this name to cover a confusing series of mid-century conflicts in Europe. Britain's part was known to the Pelhams as "The War Begun with Spain in 1739 and with France in 1744". The Austrians were more concerned about their simultaneous war with Prussia over Silesia. The Pelhams formed their administration in the middle of the War, coming to power partly because of the unpopularity of the War, and had to find an acceptable, if not conclusive, way to stop the conflict.

481. Browning, Reed. *The War of the Austrian Succession*. New York: St. Martin's Press, 1993.

482.   Anderson, M. S. *The War of the Austrian Succession, 1740-1748.* London: Longman, 1995.

These volumes are the first modern histories of the War, a fact due no doubt to the difficulties of doing research on so many participants. Both books are well written and give excellent overviews of the conflicts. Anderson's is shorter and more a textbook. Browning's is more detailed on all points, including battles.

483.   Pares, Richard. "American versus Continental War, 1739-63." *English Historical Review* 51 (1936): 429-465.

The seminal work on the conflict in British thought and policy over whether efforts should be directed to continental war or suppressing French trade at sea while attacking her position in America.

484.   Lodge, Sir Richard. *Great Britain and Prussia in the Eighteenth Century.* Oxford: Clarendon Press, 1923.

485.   Lodge, Sir Richard. *Studies in Eighteenth-Century Diplomacy 1740-1748.* London: Murray, 1930.

Lodge was the leading British diplomatic historian in the 1920s and 1930s and was a master of narrative in both style and summation. Unfortunately, he seems to have done no research in continental archives. These volumes were the chief histories of the War until Browning (481).

486.   Fayle, C. E. "Economic Pressure in the War of 1739-48." *Journal of the Royal United Service Institution* 68 (1923): 424-446.

This study of the impact of war on the volume of the combatants' trade is still useful, but Fayle misjudges British naval policy and the country's capacity for sea war.

487.   Niedhart, Gottfried. *Handel und Krieg in der britischen Weltpolitik 1738-1763.* Munich: Wilhelm Fink Verlag, 1979.

An examination of the influence of mercantilism on British war aims and Newcastle's policies as Secretary of State.

488.   Pares, Richard. *Colonial Blockade and Neutral Rights 1739-1763.* Oxford: Clarendon Press, 1938.

Useful for Newcastle's opinions on questions about prizes and relations with neutral countries, especially the Dutch.

489. Hildner, E. G. "The Role of the South Sea Company in the Diplomacy Leading to the War of Jenkins' Ear 1729-1739." *Hispanic American Historical Review* 18 (1938): 322-341.

Hildner explains the Company's dispute with Spain over South American trade and its interference in Newcastle's negotiations with Madrid to reach a financial settlement.

490. Temperley, H. W. "The Cause of the War of Jenkins' Ear, 1739." *Transactions of the Royal Historical Society* 3rd ser. 3 (1909): 197-236.

A old but still interesting account of Newcastle's negotiations with Spain on eve of war. Despite this appellation, the forcible removal of Captain Jenkins' ear did not precipitate the war.

491. Legge, L. Wickham. "Newcastle and the Counter Orders to Admiral Haddock, March 1739." *English Historical Review* 46 (1931): 272-274.

Legge absolves Newcastle of responsibility for worsening relations by ordering Haddock to continue cruising off the coast of Spain.

492. Pares, Richard. *War and Trade in the West Indies 1739-1763*. Oxford: Clarendon Press, 1936.

The standard work on British relations with France and Spain in that region. Pares notes Newcastle's opinions on many of the issues involved.

493. Harding, Richard. *Amphibious Warfare in the Eighteenth Century: The British Expedition to the West Indies 1740-1742*. London: Royal Historical Society, 1991.

Harding provides good background on the politics behind the expedition and Newcastle's part in planning it. The combined naval-military operation was not as successful as hoped and was a source of controversy and recrimination.

494. Lodge, Richard. "The So-Called Treaty of Hanau of 1743" and "The Hanau Controversy in 1744 and the Fall of Carteret." *English Historical Review* 38 (1923): 384-407 and 509-531.

Lodge analyzes how Carteret's failure to satisfy Austria for her loss of Silesia aroused the opposition of the Pelhams and led to Carteret's being forced to resign.

495.   Williams, Basil. "Carteret and the so-called Treaty of Hanau." *English Historical Review* 49 (1934): 684-687.

Williams disputes Lodge's conclusion (494) on why Carteret agreed to the Regency's rejection of a subsidy to the German emperor.

496.   Mimler, Manfred. *Der Einfluss kolonialer Interessen in Nordamerika auf die Strategie und Diplomatie Grossbritanniens während des Österreich-ischen Erbfolgekrieges 1744-1748.* Hildesheim: Georg Olms Verlag, 1983.

A meticulous study that examines the Pelham brothers' reasons for resigning in 1746 and the influence of the concept of empire on Newcastle's policies.

497.   Lodge, Richard. "The Mission of Henry Legge to Berlin, 1748." *Transactions of the Royal Historical Society* 4th ser. 14 (1931) 1-38.

Domestic political pressure, reinforced by his brother's urging, induced Newcastle to offer Frederick II the possibility of alliance with Britain. See Kulisheck (435) for a revised account.

D. THE SEVEN YEARS WAR

The 1748 Treaty of Aix-la-Chapelle only papered over the differences between the great European powers, leaving them to fester and break open again in 1754. Lacking his brother to manage Commons and no longer Secretary of State, Newcastle led a ministry responsible to an old King who remained the arbiter despite his failing health. While old studies have shown Pitt as the sole architect of victory, modern studies reduce him to his true role and demonstrate the importance of the great sums raised by Newcastle to finance the war.

498.   Middleton, Richard. *The Bells of Victory: The Pitt-Newcastle Ministry and the Conduct of the Seven Years' War, 1757-1762.* Cambridge: Cambridge University Press, 1985.

This examination of how individual departments contributed to the war effort dispels the old myth of Pitt's absolute control and clarifies how essential Newcastle's role was to victory. Success was due, Middleton points out, to having truly able men at the head of each department.

499.   Middleton, C. R. "The Administration of Newcastle and Pitt: The Departments of State and the Conduct of the Seven Years War, 1757-60." Ph.D. thesis, University of Exeter, 1968.

500. Fraser, E.J.S. "The Pitt-Newcastle Coalition and the Conduct of the Seven Years' War 1757-1760." Ph.D. thesis, Oxford University, 1976.

Fraser traces the evolution of policy and the effects of war events and political developments on policy. He examines the range of possibilities open to the coalition when they took office and Pitt's use of his outstanding ability as a politician to ensure that political factors deflected to the minimum extent the course of the war policy he wanted to follow.

501. Schweizer, Karl. "The Seven Years' War: A System Perspective" in Jeremy Black, ed., *The Origins of War in Early Modern Europe*, pp. 242-260. Edinburgh: John Donald, 1987.

Although Britain and France were the chief antagonists in the war, most of the other European countries were involved as allies of one or the other. Schweizer outlines the previous relations and present inducements that drew Prussia, Austria, and Russia into the conflict. He also criticizes Newcastle's handling of relations with Austria.

502. Baxter, Stephen. "The Conduct of the Seven Years War" in Baxter, ed., *England's Rise to Greatness, 1660-1763*, pp. 323-348. Berkeley: University of California Press, 1983.

Baxter's analysis of the political maneuvering within the ministry is rather heavy-handed and not always accurate but is does include a spirited defense of George II as a leader and administrator.

503. Browning, Reed. "The Duke of Newcastle and the Financing of the Seven Years' War." *Journal of Economic History* 31 (1971): 344-377.

Browning concludes that Newcastle managed the Treasury well because he had the confidence of the moneyed interest (the wealthiest financiers) and sought advice from able men.

504. Browning, Reed. "The Duke of Newcastle and the Financial Management of the Seven Years War in Germany." *Journal of the Society for Army Historical Research* 49 (1971): 20-35.

The Duke demanded honesty of the intermediaries who contracted with the Treasury to deliver pay, provisions, and forage to the Army, but compliance was spotty. Despite Newcastle's attempts to reform the Commissariat, a shortage of trained personnel and the problems of delivery using only wind and horse power undercut efforts at containing expenditures.

505. Little, H. M. "The Emergence of a Commissariat During the Seven Years War in Germany." *Journal of the Society for Army Historical Research* 61 (1983-1984): 201-214.

Little contends that the Newcastle Treasury Board's measures to reform the methods of feeding, clothing, arming, and paying soldiers and providing forage for the Army's horses were more successful than Browning (504) suggests. Little analyzes the organization of the system of supply and laments that Bute and Grenville destroyed the Board's nascent Commissariat, which had to be recreated for the American war.

506. Little, H. M. "The Treasury, the Commissariat and the Supply of the Combined Army in Germany During the Seven Years War (1756-1763)." Ph.D. thesis, University College, London, 1981.

A detailed examination of the cost and difficulty of supplying the Army, which was a constant anxiety for Newcastle.

507. Eldon, C. W. *England's Subsidy Policy Towards the Continent During the Seven Years' War*. Philadelphia: University of Pennsylvania Press, 1938.

Newcastle's preference for subsidies to allies burdened Pelham in his effort to reduce debt and spending. When at the Treasury himself, the Duke found his policy expensive but ultimately successful.

508. Schweizer, Karl. *England, Prussia and the Seven Years War: Studies in Alliance Politics and Diplomacy*. Lewiston: Mellen, 1989.

509. Schweizer, Karl. *Frederick the Great, William Pitt, and Lord Bute: The Anglo-Prussian Alliance, 1756-1763*. New York: Garland, 1991.

These two volumes are reassessments of the development and dissolution of the alliance and are based in part on research in the Prussian archives. Schweizer offers new views of the roles played by Newcastle, Pitt, and, in particular, Bute.

510. Middleton, Richard. "Naval Administration in the Age of Pitt and Anson, 1755-1763" in Jeremy Black and Philip Woodfine, eds., *The British Navy and the Use of Naval Power in the Eighteenth Century*, pp. 109-127. Atlantic Highlands, NJ: Humanities Press, 1989.

George Anson became allied to the Pelhams when he married Hardwicke's daughter in 1748 and was appointed First Lord of the Admiralty in both the brothers' administrations. Middleton recounts the reforms and innovations made by Anson's Admiralty Board and how they contributed to the victories of 1759.

511. Gradish, Stephen. *The Manning of the British Navy during the Seven Years' War*. London: Royal Historical Society, 1980.

Gradish claims that Pelham's parsimony in peacetime was the source of naval weakness in wartime and comments on Newcastle's relations with his Admiralty chief Anson.

512. Corbett, J. S. *England in the Seven Years' War: A Study in Combined Strategy*. London: Longmans, 1918. 2d ed. 2 vols.

This early study of what Corbett, a naval historian, calls "Pitt's war" is still useful on battles and tactics but gives a false picture of Newcastle's role.

513. Tunstall, Brian. *Admiral Byng*. London: Allan, 1928.

With both the King and the mob demanding execution, Newcastle was in no position to save the Admiral. Tunstall, a naval historian, does not understand this point and is highly critical of the Duke in this outdated defense of Byng's role in the fall of Minorca in 1756.

514. Hackmann, Kent. "The British Raid on Rochefort, 1757." *Mariner's Mirror* 64 (1978): 263-275.

Hackmann explains Newcastle's strategic and financial objections to the mounting of the raid. Pitt believed such incursions on the coast of France would keep the enemy off balance.

515. Pargellis, Stanley. *Lord Loudoun in North America*. New Haven: Yale University Press, 1948.

This study of the career of a British general provides insight into Newcastle's thinking on colonial defense before 1756.

516. Riker, T. W. "The Politics Behind Braddock's Expedition." *American Historical Review* 13 (1907-1908): 742-752.

Riker traces the origin of the Fox-Cumberland faction's opposition in 1754 to Newcastle's policies for America. A more recent assessment can be found Luff (364).

517.   Savelle, Max. *The Diplomatic History of the Canadian Boundary, 1749-1763*. New Haven: Yale University Press, 1940.

Newcastle's deep distrust of France inhibited negotiations over North America. This study explains the issues involved from both the French and the British viewpoint.

518.   Carter, Alice Clare. *The Dutch Republic in Europe in the Seven Years War*. London: Macmillan, 1971.

The sometime ally worried Newcastle because both Britain and France tried to control Dutch foreign policy. Moreover, the Dutch found investing in the British National Debt a better bargain than paying for soldiers and supplies.

519.   Schweizer, Karl. "The Cabinet Crisis of August 1761." *Bulletin of the Institute for Historical Research* 59 (1986): 225-229.

This article explains how the Duke of Devonshire negotiated with George III, Bute, Bedford, and Newcastle to smooth over differences about peace talks with France.

520.   Schweizer, Karl. "The Bedford Motion and House of Lords Debate 5 February 1762." *Parliamentary History* 5 (1986): 107-123.

Schweizer describes Newcastle's reaction to the Duke of Bedford's plan to end the German war.

521.   Schweizer, Karl. "Bute, Newcastle, Prussia and the Hague Overtures: a re-examination." *Albion* 9 (1977): 72-97.

An analysis of Newcastle's reasons for promoting an attempt in early 1762 to conciliate Austria and the reaction of Frederick II.

10

Portraits, Satires, and Poems

PORTRAITS

Although a considerable number of portraits of the Pelham brothers exist, they were executed by only a few artists. Many are copies of work done by William Hoare, a popular portrait painter in the 1750s, who may have flattered his subjects in his execution. Pelham's eyes are painted blue or blue-gray. Newcastle's are dark gray in (524). The heavy dark eyebrows given both imply black or dark brown hair (perhaps turned gray) under their wigs. Pelham appears portly in the Eccardt portraits. Newcastle was said to be taller than average and, in cartoons, was drawn very slender. Descriptions and more details on some paintings listed below and some now lost can be found in John F. Kerslake, *National Portrait Gallery Early Georgian Portraits* (London: NPG, 1977). Of the portraits, only those in the NPG are readily open to the public. Many engravings made from these portraits are listed in *Catalogue of Engraved British Portraits* (London: British Museum Trustees, 1908-1925), v.3, pp. 324-325 and 436-437, and v.6, pp. 310 and 329.

522. Newcastle, seated at a table drinking with his brother-in-law the 7th Earl of Lincoln, by Sir Godfrey Kneller, c. 1718. NPG. One in a commissioned set of portraits by Kneller of Kit-Cat Club members.

523. Newcastle, standing in peer's parliamentary robes and Garter collar and holding the Lord Chamberlain's white wand, by Kneller, c. 1720. Location unknown.

524. Newcastle, head and shoulders, with Garter ribbon and star, drawing in chalks by Hoare, c. 1752. NPG.

525. Newcastle, three-quarter length, seated in Garter robes, by Hoare, c.

1752. Palace of Westminster Art Collection. Whole-length version at Letton Hall, Norfolk.

526. Newcastle, standing in Garter robes, by Hoare. NPG on loan to Foreign Office. Another at Grundisburgh, Suffolk.

527. Newcastle by John Shackleton, Honingham Hall, Norfolk, and by an unknown artist, Buckingham Palace (no descriptions available).

528. Newcastle and Pelham, separate right profile busts modelled in wax by Isaac Gosset in 1750s. Destroyed 1994 by a fire at Uppark House, Surrey. Photo in McCann (174).

529. Pelham at age 21, head and shoulders, in armor. Engraving printed in Coxe, *Walpole* (336).

530. Pelham, three-quarter length, seated in his Chancellor of the Exchequer's gown, holding a rolled paper in his left hand, by Hoare, c. 1752. Palace of Westminster Art Collection.

531. Pelham, seated in the Chancellor's gown, by Hoare. NPG.

532. Pelham, seated in private dress, with his secretary John Roberts. Painted at Esher by Shackleton, c. 1752. NPG.

533. Pelham, seated in the Chancellor's gown, by Shackleton. NPG on loan to Government Art Collection.

534. Pelham, seated in the Chancellor's gown, with Roberts, attributed to Shackleton. Government Art Collection, Old Treasury Board Room, Whitehall.

535. Pelham, half length in the Chancellor's gown, possibly by John Giles Eccardt. Government Art Collection, 10 Downing Street.

536. Pelham, half length in private dress, very similar to (535) and possibly by Eccardt. Government Art Collection, Old Treasury Board Room, Whitehall.

537. Pelham, whole length, in blue embroidered coat, attributed to Hoare. Government Art Collection.

538. Pelham, three-quarter length, holding a paper in his right hand, attributed to Hoare. Government Art Collection.

SATIRES

As leaders of administrations, the Pelhams were obvious targets for political cartoonists. Many of these prints are preserved in the British Museum's large collection, which has been catalogued and microfilmed. The Pierpont Morgan Library, New York City, also has a collection, and the holdings of the Lewis Walpole Library, Farmington, Connecticut, almost equal the Museum's.

539. Stephens, Frederick G., and M. D. George. *Catalogue of Political and Personal Satires Preserved in the Department of Prints and Drawings in the British Museum.* London: Museum Trustees, 1870-1954. 12 vols. Set reprinted 1978.

See v.2, 1689-1733; v.3 (in 2 parts), 1734-1750 and 1750-1760; v.4, 1761-1770. Very full descriptions are given for each print but no illustrations. Chadwyck-Healey has microfilmed the *Catalogue.*

540. *English Cartoons and Satirical Prints 1320-1832 in the British Museum.* Microfilm published in 1986 by Chadwyck-Healey and held by the Center for Research Libraries, Chicago.

The drawings are numbered and arranged chronologically on 21 reels in the order given in the *Catalogue* (539).

541. Atherton, H. M. *Political Prints in the Age of Hogarth: A Study in the Ideographic Representation of Politics.* Oxford: Clarendon Press, 1974.

This study of the mid-century covers all aspects of print production, content, and audience and includes invaluable descriptions and reproductions of prints portraying the Pelhams. It also includes a section on pamphlets, which sometimes contained illustrations.

542. George, M. Dorothy. *English Political Caricature to 1792: A Study of Opinion and Propaganda.* Oxford: Clarendon Press, 1959.

George describes several cartoons lampooning Newcastle and one of Pelham. Prints of some of the cartoons described are included.

543. Brewer, John. *The Common People and Politics 1750-1790.* Cambridge: Chadwyck-Healey, 1986.

544. Dickinson, H. T. *Caricatures and the Constitution 1760-1832*. Cambridge: Chadwyck-Healey, 1986.

545. Langford, Paul. *Walpole and the Robinocracy*. Cambridge: Chadwyck-Healey, 1986.

These three volumes were issued in conjunction with the microfilm (540) and are useful introductions for persons using it, although they appear to contain nothing about the Pelhams. Cartoons were selected from the collection to illustrate the topic of the title. Each author provides a substantial essay on his topic and other material, such as the early history of political cartoons.

546. Trefman, Simon. *Sam. Foote, Comedian, 1720-1777*. New York: New York University Press, 1971.

In his 1763 farce about electioneering, *The Mayor of Garratt*, Foote imitated Newcastle's characteristic habits, such as holding a person's head between his hands while speaking to him.

547. Smollett, Tobias. *The Expedition of Humphrey Clinker*. Thomas Preston, ed. Athens: University of Georgia Press, 1990. *The History and Adventures of an Atom*. Robert Adams Day, ed. Athens: University of Georgia Press, 1989.

This novelist was less kind than even Horace Walpole in his portrayals of Newcastle. In *Clinker*, Smollett's character attends the Duke's levee and later ridicules his speech and behavior (pp. 107-112). In *Atom*, that unit circulates in the bodies of politicians, analyzing them along the way. Its description of Newcastle as an ignorant fool is cruel and insulting (pp. 12-18).

POEMS

Poems could be satirical attacks on a politician or sycophantic praises designed to earn or keep a patron. The Pelhams attracted both kinds, as can be seen in the list below. Most first appeared in pamphlet form and are included in the Eighteenth-Century Short-Title Catalogue microfilm set (see the introduction to Chapter 5). Where known, those references are given in the entry.

548. Garth, Sir Samuel. *Claremont. Address'd to the Right Honourable the Earl of Clare*. London: 1715. STC reel 4961, #14.

A pedestrian panegyric to Pelham-Holles and his estate.

549. Eusden, Lawrence. *A Poem on the Marriage of His Grace the Duke of Newcastle to the Right Honourable the Lady Henrietta Godolphin, inscrib'd to His Grace.* London: 1717. STC reel 2735, #9.

550. Moore, Edward. "The Discovery: An Ode to the Right Honourable Henry Pelham" and "The Humble Petition of the Worshipful Company of Poets and News-Writers" in his *Poems, Fables, and Plays*, pp. 1-6 and 36-38. London: Dodsley, 1756.

Both poems praise Pelham, Moore's patron. The second is a humorous complaint that Pelham conducted public affairs so well that the petitioners had nothing to write about.

551. *The Works of the Right Honourable Sir Charles Hanbury Williams, K.B.* [Annotated by Horace Walpole.] London: Jeffery, 1822. 3 vols.

"The Duke of Newcastle: A Fable" (v.1, pp. 1-13), with notes by Walpole, praises Fox and slanders the Duke as the lion who ate all previous fellow Secretaries. "An Ode to the Right Hon. Henry Pelham on his being appointed First Commissioner of the Treasury" in 1743 (v.2, pp. 71-73) is puffy praise. "The Interview between the Right Hon. Henry Pelham and William, Earl of Bath" (v.2, pp. 198-199) is a short, funny rhyme about Pelham succeeding Wilmington. An uncomplimentary note by Walpole is appended, and more are scattered throughout the volumes.

552. *The Poetical Works of David Garrick.* New York: Blom, 1968 facsimile reprint of 1785 ed. 2 vols.

Garrick's *An Ode on the Death of Mr. Pelham* was first issued as a pamphlet (London: Cooper, 1754) and reprinted several times. It is most accessible here in v.1, pp. 3-7. Garrick also wrote two stanzas entitled "Pelham, Proceed, Tho' Factions's Brood" (undated), which he allowed Moore to incorporate into a poem addressed to Pelham. Moore borrowed another stanza from Garrick to conclude his poem "The Discovery." "Death and the Devil," which Garrick wrote to celebrate Pelham's recovery from illness in 1748, exists only in manuscript. Complete information can be found in Mary Knapp, *A Checklist of Verse by David Garrick* (Charlottesville: University of Virginia Press, 1955).

553. Cibber, Colley. *Verses to the memory of Mr. Pelham.* London: 1754.

554. Jones, Henry, of Drogheda. *Verses to His Grace the Duke of Newcastle, on the death of the Right Honourable Henry Pelham.* London: 1754. STC reel 2068, #8.

555. *The Triumph of Death. A Poem in memory of the Right Honourable Henry Pelham. Imitated from Petrarch.* London: 1754. STC reel 1176, #4.

11

Places Associated with the Pelhams

Newcastle purchased the small villa Claremont, near Esher, Surrey, from the architect Sir John Vanbrugh in 1711. In the following years, the house was much enlarged by Vanbrugh and the grounds were redesigned by William Kent. While the estate provided a magnificently ducal setting, the expense of construction and maintenance drained the Duke's income.

556. Jackson-Stops, Gervase. *An English Arcadia 1600-1990*. Washington, D.C.: American Institute of Architects Press, 1991.

Engravings of the Claremont estate in 1738 and 1750 are printed on pp. 14-15 and 58-60.

557. Sedgwick, Romney. "The Duke of Newcastle's Cook." *History Today* 5 (1955): 308-316.

This story of Newcastle's search in 1754 for a good French cook gives a glimpse of his life style and explains what aristocrats wanted in and from a cook. The article includes a menu of many dishes from a 1761 dinner, a cartoon of Newcastle with his cook, a painting of Claremont, and (in error) a portrait of the 2nd Duke.

Newcastle inherited his London home, Newcastle House in Lincoln's Inn Fields, from his uncle. It was the center of Whig political activity c. 1740-1765.

558. Pearce, David. *London's Mansions*. London: Batsford, 1986.

The author provides a brief description and an engraving of Newcastle House (pp. 45-46).

559. Thornbury, George W., and Edward Walford. *Old and New London: A Narrative of Its History, Its People, and Its Places*. London: Cassell, 1873-1878. 6 vols.

This gossipy, typically Victorian set was reissued several times. Engravings and descriptions of the houses in Lincoln's Inn Fields, including Newcastle House, are printed in v.3, pp. 36-50. Areas adjacent to the Fields, the largest square in central London, also are described, including Clare Market, which Newcastle inherited from his uncle. Similar descriptive material can be found in other older histories of London, although none should be trusted as historically accurate.

Pelham, like his brother, had both a town and a country house. He purchased Esher Place, near Claremont, in 1729 and had Kent design a comfortable retreat surrounded by a landscape garden. Kent also redesigned 22 Arlington Street, the London house Pelham purchased in 1740.

560. Campbell, Peter, ed. *A House in Town: 22 Arlington Street, Its Owners and Builders*. London: Batsford, 1984.

This lavishly illustrated volume focuses on the architectural history of the house, now restored to Kent's design. Included are many photos of the interior and exterior and an account of its decoration and contents in Pelham's lifetime. Also included are engravings of Esher Place (pp. 88-90), Claremont (pp. 72-75, 92-94), and the Pelham family homes in Sussex: Halland Place (p. 70), Stanmer (p. 77), and Laughton Place (p. 91).

561. Symes, Michael. "The Landscaping of Esher Place." *Journal of Garden History* 8 (1988): 63-96.

The article includes a history of Esher Place, maps and engravings of the estate and house, a description of Kent's work, a number of his drawings, some of the expenses incurred, and a portrait of Pelham with his secretary painted at Esher (p. 71). Symes quotes from several poems that praised Esher and Pelham.

562. Smith, L. B. "The Pelham Vault." *The Sussex County Magazine* 4 (1930): 370-372.

The entrance to the vault, in the crypt of Laughton Parish Church, was sealed in 1886 after an attempted robbery aimed at jewelry buried with the bodies. A survey of the coffins taken at that time includes the inscriptions from those of the Pelham brothers, their parents and wives, their sister Frances, Pelham's daughters, and many Stanmer Pelhams. The article also includes an eyewitness account of Newcastle's burial procession and the memorial inscription for his mother within the church sanctuary.

12

Ideology and Historiography

The settlement agreed between Parliament and the new monarchs William and Mary after the Glorious Revolution of 1688 formed the basis of the English constitution. This body of principles by which the state was governed was not written down in a single document but in a series of Acts of Parliament which apportioned power among the parts of the government. The ideological dispute that inspired the Revolution, evolving with changed circumstances, continued to fuel political differences in the eighteenth century. The Pelhams often said their actions were governed by Whig principles. The works listed below throw light on what they meant.

563. Williams, E. Neville. *The Eighteenth-Century Constitution 1688-1815: Documents and Commentary*. Cambridge: Cambridge University Press, 1960.

This collection of illustrative quotations from documents and letters is divided into five sections: the Revolution, central government, Parliament, local government, and the Church, the last three being subdivided topically. Chapter introductions explain how each constituent functioned, and Williams points out how the balance of power within the central government differed from the modern British system. Quotations from and about the Pelhams are included among the illustrations for each chapter but the first.

564. Dickinson, H. T. *Liberty and Property: Political Ideology in Eighteenth-Century Britain*. London: Weidenfeld and Nicolson, 1977.

One of the long-running arguments among historians of this period is whether and to what degree political distinctions changed from Whig-Tory to Court-Country. Initially, Whigs and Tories divided ideologically over the nature of the constitution, while Court and Country divisions arose over the working of the constitution. Dickinson examines the history of the four ideological viewpoints and their development over the century.

565. Burtt, Shelley. *Virtue Transformed: Political Argument in England, 1688-1740.* Cambridge: Cambridge University Press, 1992.

An examination of concepts of civic virtue put forward by various writers of the period. Burtt distinguishes between publicly and privately oriented political virtue in the motives and character traits these writers ascribed to the good citizen. Of special interest are chapters on writers who supported the Walpole ministry's Court and Whig viewpoint and on Henry St. John, Viscount Bolingbroke, who argued on Tory and Country lines. This work is a convenient short introduction to issues explored at greater length and depth by specialists in political philosophy, whose works are listed in Burtt's bibliography.

566. Gunn, J.A.W. *Factions No More: Attitudes to Party in Government and Opposition in Eighteenth-Century England.* London: Cass, 1972.

This collection of extracts taken primarily from contemporary newspapers and pamphlets quotes examples of opinions about the existence of parties.

567. Langford, Paul. *Public Life and the Propertied Englishman 1689-1798.* Oxford: Clarendon Press, 1991.

Langford examines assumptions about the theory and practice of politics, and two in particular: that property conferred authority and that government should be conducted by men at the top of the social order. He asks "how did propertied society respond to the demands made by economic growth, commercial competition, and social change, in respect of the exercise of public responsibility?" To find answers Langford looks into public life rather than private affairs, that is, into men's participation in governmental and voluntary associations. He searches down to the local level and to the middle class, looking for the forces that unite all persons of property.

568. Dickinson, H. T. *The Politics of the People in Eighteenth-Century Britain.* New York: St. Martin's Press, 1995.

The introduction is a review of various historians' interpretations of eighteenth-century British politics and views on oligarchical rule. Dickinson then examines the ways the public at large could influence politics and how ordinary people became politicized over the century. This work is a good companion to be read with Langford (566).

569. Browning, Reed. *Political and Constitutional Ideas of the Court Whigs.* Baton Rouge: Louisiana State University Press, 1982.

Browning examines the historical and philosophical origins of Whig ideology and its evolution in the Walpole and Pelham eras. Five men who were friends or colleagues of the Pelhams are used as examples of this ideology in action: the courtier Lord Hervey, Bishop Benjamin Hoadly, Archbishop Thomas Herring, historian and clergyman Samuel Squire, and Lord Chancellor Hardwicke. As Newcastle's long-time friend and chief advisor, Hardwicke influenced policy far beyond his official sphere as head of the legal system.

570. Colley, Linda. *In Defiance of Oligarchy: The Tory Party 1714-1760.* Cambridge: Cambridge University Press, 1982.

This work has been much criticized for finding a party where one did not exist, although it is difficult to judge how much of the criticism arises from historians' personal bias. See Thomas (574) for an example. Even if no coherent party existed, men whom the Pelhams called Tories certainly did. As the only modern history of Tory politics, this work supplies information on ideology, activities, and voting which is hard to find elsewhere.

571. Brewer, John. *Party Ideology and Popular Politics at the Accession of George III.* Cambridge: Cambridge University Press, 1976.

Brewer examines pamphlets and other expressions of popular opinion for evidence of changing political thought in a period of political instability. This study is useful on Whig ideology.

572. Peters, Marie. "'Names and Cant': Party Labels in English Political Propaganda *c.* 1755-1765." *Parliamentary History* 3 (1984): 103-127.

Peters points out that the continued use of party labels at a time when the old Whig and Tory parties supposedly were disintegrating testifies to the ideological power inherent in these labels.

Like the Pelhams and their contemporaries, modern historians of eighteenth-century Britain quarrel over ideology, criticizing each other's work and sometimes resorting to personal insults. The following works shed some light on how historians' viewpoints may have affected their interpretation of events.

573. Colley, Linda. "The Politics of Eighteenth-Century British History." *Journal of British Studies* 25 (1986): 359-379.

Colley uses this literature review to point out the difficulties facing historians writing about the eighteenth century and describes the viewpoints adopted by some prominent historians. She cites three phases of twentieth-century historiography about eighteenth-century Britain: Namierism; reaction to Namierism coinciding with a revival of interest in social history; the new orthodoxy. For Namier, see (576).

574.   Thomas, P.D.G. "Party Politics in Eighteenth-Century Britain: Some Myths and a Touch of Reality." *British Journal for Eighteenth-Century Studies* 10 (1987): 201-211.

Thomas also looks at Namierism and the reaction to it and reviews historians' arguments for and against the existence of a significant Tory party. Thomas presents his own reasons against existence and criticizes the supporters, Colley in particular, quite harshly.

575.   Black, Jeremy. "Eighteenth-Century English Politics: Recent Work and Current Problems." *Albion* 25 (1993): 419-441.

In this literature review, Black disputes some of Thomas' criticisms and offers his own opinions on the political viewpoints of various historians.

576.   Colley, Linda. *Lewis Namier*. London: Weidenfeld and Nicolson, 1989.

Sir Lewis was perhaps the most influential historian of eighteenth-century Britain, known especially for founding the *History of Parliament* project. In this biography, Colley describes how Namier challenged the old "Whig interpretation" of parliamentary politics as conducted on a simple two-party basis.

13

Bibliographies and
Guides to Further Materials

Some of the works listed here are rather old but still useful for finding material about the Pelham era. The annual publications are more up-to-date, reviewing material published one or two years earlier. Readers will find it profitable to look through the bibliographies of the volumes listed in Chapter 14 for recent work on particular topics.

577. Pargellis, Stanley, and D. J. Medley. *Bibliography of British History: The Eighteenth Century, 1714-1789.* Oxford: Clarendon Press, 1951.

578. Gipson, L. H. *Bibliographic Guide to the History of the British Empire, 1748-1776.* New York: Knopf, 1969.

579. Elton, G. R. *Modern Historians on British History, 1485-1945: A Critical Bibliography, 1945-1969.* Ithaca: Cornell University Press, 1971.

580. Schlatter, Richard, ed. *Recent Views on British History: Essays on Historical Writing Since 1966.* New Brunswick: Rutgers University Press, 1984.

581. Richardson, R. C., and W. H. Chaloner, eds. *British Economic and Social History: A Bibliographic Guide.* Manchester: Manchester University Press, 1996. 3rd ed.

582. Norton, Mary Beth, ed. *American Historical Association's Guide to Historical Literature.* New York: Oxford University Press, 1995. 3rd ed.

583. *Writings on British History.* London: Royal Historical Society, 1901-

1974. Continued as *Annual Bibliography of British and Irish History*. London: Royal Historical Society, 1975-1986 and 1991-   .

The bibliographic essays are divided into historical periods and cover both books and articles.

584. *Annual Bulletin of Historical Literature*. London: Historical Association, 1911-   .

Bibliographic essays covering both books and articles are divided by time periods and subdivided by topics.

585. Mullins, E.L.C. *Texts and Calendars: An Analytical Guide to Serial Publications*. London: Royal Historical Society, 1978 corrected reprint.

586. Mullins, E.L.C. *Texts and Calendars II: An Analytical Guide to Serial Publications 1957-1982*. London: Royal Historical Society, 1983.

These companion volumes list the contents of publications relating to British history issued in collections or series by official bodies or private societies.

587. Stevenson, David and Wendy. *Scottish Texts and Calendars: An Analytical Guide to Serial Publications*. London: Royal Historical Society, 1987.

This guide covers works relating to Scotland issued by private societies.

588. *Historical Abstracts, Part A, 1450-1914*. Santa Barbara: American Bibliographic Center, ongoing.

Available in print and on CD-ROM. Both books and articles are included and are arranged by geographical area and time period. Not every relevant journal is included in this survey.

589. *Dissertation Abstracts*. Ann Arbor: University Microfilms, ongoing.

Available in print and on CD-ROM.

590. *Index to Theses with Abstracts Accepted for Higher Degrees by the Universities of Great Britain and Ireland and the Council for National Academic Awards*. London: Aslib, 1950-   .

Abstracts were not included in this index until v.35 (November 1986). Available on CD-ROM for 1970 onward.

591. Fryde, E. B., et al., eds. *Handbook of British Chronology*. London: Royal Historical Society, 1986. 3rd ed.

The volume is a compilation of lists of office holders and other sorts of appointees in Britain and Ireland from earliest times.

592. Cornish, Rory. *George Grenville 1712-1770: A Bibliography*. Westport: Greenwood Press, 1992.

593. Schweizer, Karl. *William Pitt, Earl of Chatham, 1708-1778: A Bibliography*. Westport: Greenwood Press, 1993.

These two compilations of material about contemporaries of the Pelhams are useful sources on particular topics.

594. *Hanoverian Britain: An Encyclopedia*. New York: Garland, 1997.

The entries cover all aspects of politics, society, and culture in the period 1714-1830 and contain small bibliographies.

595. *A Dictionary of Eighteenth-Century World History*. Jeremy Black and Roy Porter, eds. Oxford: Blackwell, 1994.

This volume includes essays on ideas, movements, and persons active in politics, the arts, and science, plus maps, a chronology, and list of further readings.

596. *The Blackwell Companion to the Enlightenment*. John Yolton, ed. Oxford: Blackwell, 1991.

The essays, with appended bibliographies, cover all aspects of intellectual inquiry and the persons pursuing them in the period 1720-1780.

14

Recent Histories
of Eighteenth-Century Britain

In the last 25 years, a great deal of research has been done on this period, leading to changed perceptions of persons and new interpretations of events. In particular, historians have looked beyond the older, more narrow story of politics to learn of changes in society and the economy. The volumes listed below differ in emphasis and intended audience, but all incorporate the results of the latest research and provide the context necessary to understanding the Pelhams.

597. Black, Jeremy, ed. *Britain in the Age of Walpole*. New York: St. Martin's Press, 1984.

598. Black, Jeremy, ed. *British Politics and Society from Walpole to Pitt 1742-1789*. New York: St. Martin's Press, 1990.

These companion volumes cover most of the century and consist of essays written by leading historians. Topics of the sections are society, the economy, Scotland and Ireland, parliamentary politics, radicals and reformers, foreign policy, the empire, and religion. Excellent topical bibliographies are included.

599. Holmes, Geoffrey, and Daniel Szechi. *The Age of Oligarchy: Pre-Industrial Britain, 1722-1783*. London: Longman, 1993.

This textbook provides a chronological outline of major events followed by a survey of the political, social, and economic situation. A compendium of statistical material includes a population table, a genealogy of the House of Hanover, lists of government officials, tables of gross national product, and similar information.

600. Langford, Paul. *A Polite and Commercial People: England 1727-1783*. Oxford: Clarendon Press, 1989.

This volume is part of the *New Oxford History of England* series. Dr. Langford is stylistically the best of current British historians and has great command of sources. His narrative alternates between the political and the social scene. A splendid bibliographic essay is appended.

601. Rule, John. *Albion's People: English Society, 1714-1815* and *The Vital Century: England's Developing Economy, 1714-1815*. London: Longman, 1992.

These companion volumes synthesize recent research on social and economic history and are divided into topical sections. Among the subjects covered are organization of labor and conditions of work, consequences of enclosure, the consumer revolution, the standard of living, popular culture, religion, crime and punishment, and the lives of persons of different classes (upper, middling, lower).

Index to Authors

All numbers cited are entry numbers except those preceded by a p., which indicates the reference appears in explanatory text on that page.

Almon, John, 234
Anderson, M. S., 422, 482
Atherton, H. M., 541
Ayling, Stanley, 349, 450

Barnes, Donald, 321, 468
Barrow, Sir John, 220
Basye, Arthur, 473
Bateson, Mary, 199, 472
Battestin, Martin and Ruth, 371
Baugh, D. A., 381, 424, 425
Baxter, Stephen, 502
Beattie, John M., 332
Beatty, J. L., 369
Bigham, Clive, 2nd Viscount Mersey, 327
Bill, E.G.W., 87
Bisset, Andrew, 186
Black, Jeremy, 176, 206, 209, 212, 297, 335, 339, 343, 350, 372, 396-401, 403, 405, 409, 411, 416, 419, 426, 428, 443, 501, 510, 575, 595, 597, 598
Blanchard, Rae, 171
Boaden, James, 201
Bond, Maurice, 86, 243
Bond, R. P., 314

Bourke, Sir Richard, 200
Brauer, Gert, 420
Brewer, John, 379-381, 543, 571
Bricke, Margaret, 368
Bromley, J. S., 418
Brooke, John, 202, 434, 449
Brown, Peter, 226
Browning, Reed, 317, 431, 432, 481, 503, 504, 569
Buffington, A. H., 477
Bullion, John, 443, 445, 453
Burtt, Shelley, 565
Bussemaker, Th., 219

Cady, Priscilla, 408
Campbell, Peter, 328, 560
Canny, Nicholas, 381
Carswell, John, 215
Carter, Alice Clare, 442, 518
Cavendish, William, 4th Duke of Devonshire, 226, 227
Chaloner, W. H., 581
Chance, J. F., 177
Chandler, Richard, 233
Christie, Ian, 204, 448
Cibber, Colley, 553
Clark, Dora Mae, 382

Clark, J.C.D., 218, 433
Clayton, T. R., 478
Cleary, Thomas, 370
Cobbett, William, 232
Colley, Linda, 570, 573, 576
Conn, Stetson, 427
Connors, Richard, 213, 354-357
Conway, Julian, p. 2
Copeland, Thomas, 231
Corbett, J. S., 512
Cornish, Rory, 294, p. 63, 592
Coxe, William, 169, 179, 320, 336
Crane, R. S., 299
Cranfield, G. A., 376
Cross, Arthur, 185, 462

Dann, Uriel, 421
Day, Robert Adams, 547
Debrett, John, 234
Dickens, Lilian, 223
Dickinson, H. T., 322, 544, 564, 568
Dickson, P.G.M., 378, 418
Ditchfield, G. M., 249
Dodington, George Bubb, 215
Dralle, L. A., 215
Dunthorne, Hugh, 404, 405

Eldon, C. W., 507
Elliott, G.F.S., 440
Elliott, J. H., 429
Ellis, Kenneth, 393
Elton, G. R., 579
Englefield, Dermot, 323
Eusden, Lawrence, 549
Evans, Charles, p. 55

Falkiner, C. Litton, 194
Fayle, C. E., 486
Fitzwilliam, The Earl, 200
Foord, Archibald, 362
Ford, Percy and Grace, 247
Foster, Janet, p. 1
Fortescue, Sir John, 197, 198

Fox, Henry, 228
Fox-Strangways, Giles, Lord Stavordale and 6th Earl of Ilchester, 184, 228, 363
Fox-Strangways, Mary, Countess of Ilchester, 228
Fraser, E.J.S., 500
Fritz, Paul, 320, 366
Fryde, E. B., 591

Garnett, Richard, 217
Garrick, David, 552
Garth, Samuel, 548
George, M. Dorothy, 539, 542
Gerrard, Christine, 346
Gerretson, C., 182
Geyl, P., 182
Gibson, William, 470, 471
Ginter, Donald, 250
Gipson, L. H., 578
Glover, Richard, 214
Gradish, Stephen, 511
Graham, John Murray, 178
Graham, Walter, 313
Greaves, R. W., 465
Griffin, Grace, 138
Gunn, J.A.W., 566

Hackmann, Kent, 514
Haffenden, Philip, 475
Hanson, Laurence, 300
Harding, Richard, 414, 493
Harris, George, 173
Harris, Michael, 296
Harris, Robert, 298, 348, 377
Hatton, Ragnhild, 331, 422
Haydon, Colin, 367
Hayton, David, 249
Henretta, James, 474
Hervey, John, Baron Hervey, 210
Hildner, E. G., 489
Hirschberg, D. R., 469
Hodgart, Matthew, 204
Holmes, Geoffrey, 599

Hoppit, Julian, 386
Horn, D. B., 100, 395, 429, 430
Howells, Catherine, 330
Hughes, Michael, 259

Ingram, K. E., 113
Innes, Joanna, 381

Jackson-Stops, Gervase, 556
Jones, Clyve, 249, 343, 456
Jones, David Lewis, 245
Jones, Henry, 554
Jucker, N. S., 230

Katz, Stanley, 476
Kaye, F. B., 299
Kelch, Ray, 318
Kemp, Betty, 345
Keppel, George, 6th Earl of
    Albemarle, 195
Kerslake, John, p. 107
Knachtbull, Sir Edward, 207
Knapp, Mary, 552
Koenigsberger, H. G., 429
Kulisheck, P. J., 435, 497

Lam, George, 204
Lambert, Sheila, 241, 242
Landsman, Ned, 381
Langford, Paul, 340, 455, 545,
    567, 600
Lawson, Philip, 221, 444
Lawson-Tancred, Sir Thomas, 170
Legge, L. Wickham, 177, 491
Lemmings, David, 374
Lewis, W. S., 204
Little, H. M., 505, 506
Lodge, Sir Richard, 180, 407, 410,
    484, 485, 494, 497
Luff, P. A., 358, 359, 364, 436
Lyttelton, George, 1st Baron
    Lyttelton, 190

Macauley, John S., 465

McCahill, Michael, 456
McCann, Timothy, 174
McCormick, Frank, 329
McKelvey, James, 439
Manning, Frederick J., 480
Mason, W., 267
Mediger, W., 422
Medley, D. J., 577
Menhennet, David, 244
Middleton, C. Richard, 498, 499,
    510
Mimler, Manfred, 496
Mitchell, Sir Andrew, 186
Moore, Edward, 550
Mullins, E.L.C., 585, 586
Mure, W., 193

Namier, Sir Lewis, 198, 388, 434,
    446, 447
Natan, Alex, 345
Newman, A. N., 207, 322, 417,
    438
Nickson, M.A.E., p. 2
Niedhart, Gottfried, 487
Norton, Mary Beth, 582
Nulle, Stebelton, 316, 338

O'Gorman, Frank, 451, 454
Olson, Alison, 464
Owen, J. B., 347, 418

Pares, Richard, 483, 488, 492
Pargellis, Stanley, 515, 577
Pearce, David, 558
Pemberton, W. Baring, 344
Percival, John, 1st Earl of Egmont,
    208
Percival, John, 2nd Earl of
    Egmont, 438
Perkins, Clarence, 342
Perry, Thomas, 375
Peters, Marie, p. 59, 301, 437,
    572
Phelps, Rose, 248

Phillimore, Robert, 190
Pike, E. Royston, 325
Plumb, J. H., 337
Poole, Robert, 373
Porter, Roy, 595
Preston, Thomas, 547
Pringle, J. H., 188

Rea, Robert, 302
Reitan, E. A., 390
Richardson, R. C., 581
Riker, T. W., 516
Roberts, R. A., p. 35
Robertson, John, 381
Rodgers, Frank, 248
Rogers, Nicholas, 387
Rose, Sir George, 189
Roseveare, Henry, 383
Rule, John, 601
Russell, Lord John, 183
Russell Barker, G. F., 203

Sainty, J. C., 361, 384, 392
Savelle, Max, 517
Schlatter, Richard, 580
Schlenke, Manfred, 423
Schweizer, Karl, 196, 226, 227,
    229, 294, p. 63, 399, 405, 443,
    445, 451-453, 501, 508, 509,
    519-521, 593
Scott, H. M., 428
Seaton, Janet, 323
Sedgwick, Romney, 204, 210, 225,
    353, 389, 557
Shaw, William, 76
Sheppard, Julia, p. 1
Shy, Arlene, p. 29
Simmons, R. C., 238
Smith, David Nichol, 175
Smith, L. B., 562
Smith, Warren, 204
Smith, William James, 192
Smollett, Tobias, 547
Spector, R. D., 303, 315

Sperling, John G., 406
Stanton, Mary, 223
Steer, Francis, 110
Stephen, Sir Leslie, 324
Stephens, F. G., 539
Stevenson, David and Wendy, 587
Stock, Leo, 237
Stone, Lawrence, 381
Sutherland, Lucy, 385
Sykes, Norman, 466, 467
Symes, Michael, 561
Szechi, Daniel, 599

Taylor, Stephen, 458-461, 463
Taylor, W. S., 188
Temperley, H. W., 479, 490
Terry, Charles, 181
Thomas, P.D.G., 238, 360, 574
Thomson, G. M., 326
Thomson, M. A., p. 59, 391
Thornbury, George W., 559
Timberland, Ebenezer, 235
Tomlinson, J.R.G., 222
Torbuck, John, 236
Torrington, F. W., 240
Trefman, Simon, 546
Tunstall, Brian, 513
Turner, Thomas, 224

Vaisey, David, 224
Vanbrugh, Sir John, 205
Van Thal, Herbert, 322
Vaucher, Paul, 211
Venables, J.E.A., 110
Viator, Timothy, 334

Waldegrave, James, 2nd Earl
    Waldegrave, 218
Walford, Edward, 559
Walpole, Horace, 202-204, 551
Watson, D. H., 457
Watt, Robert, p. 55
Webb, Geoffrey, 205
White, Isobel, 323

Whiteman, Anne, 418
Whitworth, Rex, 365
Wilkes, John, 319
Williams, Basil, 341, 394, 495
Williams, Sir Charles Hanbury, 551
Williams, David, 320
Williams, E. Neville, 563
Wilson, A. M., 402
Wilson, Charles, 441
Wilson, Kathleen, 381

Winstanley, D. A., 352
Winton, Calhoun, 333
Woodfine, Philip, 412, 413, 415, 426, 510
Wrigley, E. A., 381
Wyndham, Maud, 191

Yolton, John, 596
Yorke, Philip, 172
Yorke, Philip, Lord Royston, 213

Index to Correspondents and Subjects

The numbers cited are entry numbers. Newcastle's letters are not listed, but, for the reader's convenience, letters to and from Pelham are indexed under his name. Peers are cross-indexed by title and surname, where known. This list does not include all the correspondents indexed in the *Catalogue* of the Newcastle Papers, but most of the names listed here do appear there.

Administrative papers, 1k-l, 1n-o

Admiralty, 60, 73

Albemarle, Earl of, *see* Keppel

Aller, Edward, 5

American colonies, 1r, 2a, 70, 88, 237, 238, 382, 462-464, 496, 515, 516

Amyand, Claudius, 66i

Anson, George, 1st Baron Anson, 10, 66c, 220, 510

Anson, Thomas, 10

Anti-Catholicism, 357

Argyll, Duke of, *see* Campbell

Armstrong, John, 137

Army, 1s, 73, 75, 77, 84, 89

Arundell, Richard, 64

Ashburnham, William, 66p

Barnard, Sir John, 66f, 66m

Barrington, William Wildman, 2nd Viscount Barrington, 4, 60

Bath, Earl of, *see* Pulteney

Bedford, Duke of, *see* Russell

Bennett, Charles, Earl of Tankerville, 66j

Bentinck, Jane, Countess Dowager of Portland, 15

Bentinck, Count Willem, 4, 20, 21, 66g-h, 182, 219

Bentinck, William Cavendish, 3rd Duke of Portland, 65

Berkeley, George, 18

Blackwell, T., 66n

Blair, David, 66m

Blakeney, William, 66-l, 89

Bland, Humphrey, 66-l, 66n-o

Board of Trade, 473

Boyle, Henry, 66k

Brand, Sir Thomas, 66m

Burke, Edmund, 200, 231

Burnet, Thomas, 175

Bury, Lord, 66h

Bute, Earl of, *see* Stuart

Byng, Admiral John, 2n, 275, 281, 282, 513

Cabinet and Privy Council, 1h,
2e, 51, 66c, 66j, 153, 221,
388, 389
Calendar Reform Act of 1752,
373
Cambridge, University of, 1bb,
2c, 3, 29, 73, 352
Cameron, Archibald, 369
Campbell, Archibald, 3rd Duke of
Argyll, 66-l, 66n-o, 72, 142,
368
Campbell, Colin, 66o
Campbell, Hugh, 3rd Earl of
Loudoun, 98, 130, 131
Campbell, James, 130
Campbell, John, 93
Campbell, John, 4th Earl of
Loudoun, 98, 131, 515
Campion, Henry, 66f
Canada, 70, 112, 517
Capel, William, 3rd Earl of
Essex, 23, 66a
Carlisle, Earl of, *see* Howard
Carmichael, John, 3rd Earl of
Hyndford, 8, 46, 66e
Carteret, John, 2nd Baron Carteret
and 2nd Earl of Granville, 17,
66c, 160, 344, 394, 494, 495
Catherwood, John, 117
Cavendish, William, 3rd Duke of
Devonshire, 81
Cavendish, William, Marquis of
Hartington and 4th Duke of
Devonshire, 66p, 81, 226,
227, 519
Cayley, William, 66e
Charterhouse, 1bb
Chatham, Earl of, *see* Pitt
Chesterfield, Earl of, *see*
Stanhope
Church patronage, 66i, 73, 87
Churchill, Charles, 66m

Churchill, John, 1st Duke of
Marlborough, 1w
Churchill, Sarah, Duchess of
Marlborough, 1w, 53, 329
Cider Tax, 37
Civil List and pensions, 11, 37,
66c, 76, 390
Claremont, 548, 556, 557
Clayton, Jasper, 142
Clevland, John, 66p
Clinton, Catherine, Lady Lincoln,
66p
Clinton, George, 115, 117
Clinton, Henry, 7th Earl of
Lincoln, 522
Clinton, Henry, 9th Earl of
Lincoln, 66, 66p, 66r
Coade, John, 66i
Coke, Thomas, Earl of Leicester,
66j, 157
Colebrooke, George, 89
Colebrooke, John, 89
Colonial Office, 70
Company of Rhode Island, 127
Cope, John, 66-l
Cornbury, Viscount, *see* Hyde
Cornwall politics, 66j, 106, 113
Cornwall, Velters, 66b
Coxe, William, 1f, 6, 66q, 320
Craggs, James, Jr., 62
Crokatt, James, 115
Cumberland, William Augustus,
Duke of, 66b, 66d-f, 66-l, 75,
364, 365, 516

D'Arcy, Sir Conyers, 66-l
Darcy, Robert, 4th Earl of
Holdernesse, 48, 66g-h
Dalrymple, John, 2nd Earl of
Stair, 2f, 2j, 75, 178
Dalrymple, William, 66m
Dartmouth, Earl of, *see* Legge

Dayrolle, James, 11, 14
Dayrolle, Solomon, 11, 66g, 143
Debates and speeches, 1h, 2o, 40, 115, 207-209, 212, 213
Denbigh, Earl of, 167
Deneken, Mons., 66g
Devonshire, Duke of, *see* Cavendish
Dicker, Michael, 66c, 115
Dinwiddie, Robert, 115, 119
Dodington, George Bubb, 215, 216
d'Oeyras, Comte, 13
Dorset, Duke of, *see* Sackville
Douglas, James, 14th Earl of Morton, 66d, 66n
Douglas, William, 3rd Earl of March, 66m
Drummond, George, 66m-o
Drury Lane Theater, 333, 334
Dundas, George, 66n
Dundas, Henry, Lord Melville, 147
Dundas, Lawrence, 66n
Dundas, Robert, 66n, 91
Dundas, Robert, Jr., 66n
Dunk, George Montagu, 2nd Earl of Halifax, 66p
Dunmore, Earl of, *see* Murray
Dupplin, Lord, *see* Hay

Earl, William, 66m
East India Company, 1r, 103
Eccardt, John Giles, 535, 536
Edgecombe, R., 66i
Edlyn, Edward, 66m, 66o
Egmont, Earl of, *see* Percival
Egremont, Earl of, *see* Wyndham
Election campaigns, 170, 338, 341, 342
Elibank Plot of 1752, 369
Elliot, Gilbert, 440

Erskine, James, 66m
Erskine, Charles, 66n, 94
Esher Place, 560, 561
Essex, Earl of, *see* Capel
Excise Crisis, 340

Fane, Henry, 6th Earl of Westmoreland, 66c
Fawkener, Sir Everard, 66d, 66-1
Ferdinand, Prince, of Brunswick, 54
Field, Edward, 80
Fielding, Henry, 370, 371
Finch, Lady Isabella, 26
Findlater, Earl, of *see* Ogilvy
FitzGerald, J., 66b
Fletcher, Andrew, 66n, 181
Fleury, Cardinal, 441
Fluyder, S., 66i
Foote, Samuel, 546
Forbes, Duncan, 66-1-n, 92
Fordyce, James, 66m
Foreign affairs, 1g, 1p-q, 2g, 5, 8, 11, 20, 23, 36, 39, 44-46, 48, 49, 66a-j, 71, 75, 82, 90, 96, 105, 123, 137, 145, 206, 343, 391-432, 452
Foreign Office, 71
Fortrose, Lord, 66-1
Fox, Henry, 1st Baron Holland, 50, 66e, 66h, 84, 135, 184, 228, 363, 364, 436, 516
Frederick, Prince of Wales, 66q, 345, 348, 438
Frederick II of Prussia, 62, 422, 423, 484, 497, 508, 509

Garrick, David, 201
George I, 331, 332
George II, 66o, 66q, 161, 372, 409, 417-422, 502
George III, 47, 66q, 197, 198,

225, 438, 439, 448-450
Germain, George Sackville, 66k, 118, 151, 152
Gerss, Philip, 80
Gibraltar, 70, 427
Gibson, Edmund, 87
Gideon, Samson, 385
Gilmour, Sir Charles, 66n
Glover, Richard, 214
Godolphin, Francis, 2nd Earl of Godolphin, 1v-w
Goodricke, Sir John, 143
Gordon, Cosmo, 3rd Duke of Gordon, 66n
Gordon, William, 17th Earl of Sutherland, 66-l, 124
Gore, J., 66b
Gosset, Isaac, 528
Gower, Earl, *see* Leveson-Gower
Graham, William, 2nd Duke of Montrose, 66-l
Granby, Marquis of, *see* Manners
Grant, Sir Ludovic, 66m-n
Granville, Earl of, *see* Carteret
Grenville, George, 192, 222, 444, 445, 592
Guilford, Earl of, *see* North

Haddock, Nicholas, 28, 491
Haldane, Patrick, 66n
Halifax, Earl of, *see* Dunk
Hampdon, Viscount, *see* Trevor
Hanover, 66j, 73, 420-422
Hardinge, Nicholas, 66k
Hardwicke, Earl of, *see* Yorke
Hardwicke's Marriage Act of 1753, 374
Hare, Francis, 162
Harley, Robert, 1st Earl of Oxford, 147, 158
Harrington, Earl of, *see* Stanhope

Hartford, Lord, 66a
Hartington, Marquis of, *see* Cavendish
Haslang, Count von, 66h
Hastings, Theophilus, 9th Earl of Huntingdon, 130, 168
Hay, John, 4th Marquis of Tweeddale, 66-l, 95
Hay, Thomas, Lord Dupplin and 8th Earl of Kinnoull, 41
Hedges, John, 104
Henley, Robert, Lord Henley and 1st Earl of Northington, 58
Herring, Archbishop Thomas, 217, 569
Hervey, John, Baron Hervey, 210, 569
Hesse, Princess of, 66g
Hibbens, Lucius, 471
Hoare, Henry, 66q
Hoare, William, p. 107, 524-526, 530, 531, 537, 538
Hoghton, Sir H., 66-l
Holdernesse, Earl of, *see* Darcy
Holland, Baron, *see* Fox
Holles, John, Duke of Newcastle, 158
Holles, Margaret, Duchess of Newcastle, 154, 158
Honeywood, Sir Philip, 142
Hope, John, 2nd Earl of Hopetoun, 66m, 99
Hosier, Francis, 61
Howard, Charles, 66-l
Howard, Charles, 3rd Earl of Carlisle, 163, 176
Howard, Henrietta, Countess of Suffolk, 18
Hume, Abraham, 66i
Hume-Campbell, Alexander, Lord Polwarth and 2nd Earl of Marchmont, 39, 108, 166

Hume-Campbell, Alexander, 66n, 166

Hume-Campbell, Hugh, 3rd Earl of Marchmont, 108, 166, 189

Hunter, Robert, 114

Hunter, Thomas Orby, 66a-b, 66f, 89, 142

Huntingdon, Earl of, *see* Hastings

Hurdis, Thomas, 1x

Huske, John, 66c, 66-l

Hyde, Henry, Viscount Cornbury and 1st Baron Hyde, 66g-h

Hyndford, Earl of, *see* Carmichael

Idle, Baron, 66n

Ireland, 66k, 74, 194

Irwin, Viscount, 66g-h, 164

Jenkinson, Charles, 40, 230

Jewish Naturalization Act of 1753, 375-377

Johnson, John, 116

Johnstone, George, 66-l

Jones, Hugh Valence, 2d

Juries Act of 1730, 372

Keene, Sir Benjamin, 45, 66a, 66d-e, 66h, 105, 115, 116, 123

Keith, Robert, 2g, 2-l, 66g, 66i

Kent, William, 560, 561

Keppel, George, 3rd Earl of Albemarle, 25

Keppel, William, 2nd Earl of Albemarle, 66c, 66f, 66h-j, 66-l, 181

Kerr, James, 66n

Kerr, Lord Mark, 66-l

Kinnoull, Earl of, *see* Hay

Kit-Cat Club, 330, 522

Knachtbull, Sir Edward, 207

Kneller, Sir Godfrey, 522, 523

Lambert, Sir Daniel, 66g

Lauderdale, Earl of, *see* Maitland

Law, Jonathan, 119

Law, The, 2a

Leeds, Duke of, *see* Osborne

Legge, Henry Bilson, 66e-f, 111, 435, 443, 497

Legge, William, 2nd Earl of Dartmouth, 156

Leicester, Earl, of *see* Coke

Leigh, Peter, 66j

Lennox, Charles, 2nd Duke of Richmond, 66b, 110, 174

Leslie, John, 9th Earl of Rothes, 66n

Lestock, Richard, 136

Leveson-Gower, John, 1st Earl of Gower, 66b, 68

Leveson-Gower, Richard, 66f

Ligonier, Sir John, 66c, 121

Lincoln, Earl of, *see* Clinton

Lincoln's Inn Fields Theater, 334

London Common Council, 387

Lonsdale, Viscount, *see* Lowther

Loudoun, Earl of, *see* Campbell

Lowther, Henry, 2nd Viscount Lonsdale, 161

Lyttelton, George, 1st Baron Lyttelton, 66f, 132, 190, 191

Mackay, George, 66n,

Mackay, George, 3rd Baron Reay, 66n

Maitland, Charles, 66n

Maitland, James, 7th Earl of Lauderdale, 66n

Manners, John, 3rd Duke of Rutland, 80

Manners, John, Marquis of Granby, 54, 66p, 159

Mansfield, Earl of, *see* Murray

March, Earl of, *see* Douglas

Marchmont, Earl of, *see* Hume-
    Campbell
Marlborough, Duke of, *see*
    Churchill
Martin, Samuel, Jr., 43
Martyn, Benjamin, 115
Mathews, Thomas, 20
Mauduit, Israel, 452
Maule, Jo., 66n
Maxwell, John, 66n
Mayance, Elector of, 66g
Melville, Lord, *see* Dundas
Microfilm and other microforms,
    pp. 1-2, 1b, 51, 73, 76, 139,
    141, 158, 232, 234, 239,
    p. 55, 294, 295, 351, 539,
    540, 543-545, p. 110
Middlesex, Lord, *see* Sackville
Miller, Sanderson, 223
Mirepoix, Duc de, 66h, 211
Mitchell, Sir Andrew, 4, 52, 186
Monson, Charles, 89
Montagu, Edward Wortley, 66f
Montagu, John, 2nd Duke of
    Montagu, 142
Montagu, John, 4th Earl of
    Sandwich, 66b, 66d-f, 96
Montrose, Duke of, *see* Graham
Mordaunt, Sir John, 66e, 66-l,
    142
Morris, Corbyn, 115
Morton, Earl, of *see* Douglas
Münchhausen, Baron G. A. von,
    66p, 69
Munro, Sir Harry, 66m
Munro, Sir Robert, 66b
Murray, John, 2nd Earl of
    Dunmore, 55, 66d
Murray, William, 1st Earl of
    Mansfield, 33, 66q, 109

Namier, Sir Lewis, 446, 447,
    573, 574, 576
Navy, 1s, 61, 73, 359, 399, 413,
    424-426, 510-513
Newcastle, Duke and Duchess of,
    see Holles and Pelham-Holles
Newcastle House, 558, 559
Nicoll, John, 142
Norris, Sir John, 19, 66g
North, Francis, 1st Earl of
    Guilford, 102
Northington, Earl of, *see* Henley
Nottingham politics, 1bb, 62
Nova Scotia, 9, 66h, 128
Nugent, Robert, 1st Earl Nugent,
    142, 143

Ogilvy, James, 6th Earl of
    Findlater, 66n
Oglethorpe, James, 66-l
O'Hara, James, 2nd Baron
    Tyrawly, 19, 66a, 66c, 66-l
Onslow, Arthur, 66q
Orange, Princess of, 66a, 66g,
    405
Ord, James, 115
Orford, Earl of, *see* Walpole
Osborne, Thomas, 4th Duke of
    Leeds, 24, 124, 142
Ossario, 66e-f
Oswald, James, 187
Oxford, Earl of, *see* Harley
Oxford, University of, 1bb

Parliament, 1g, 1i, 1n, 2o, 73,
    86, 232-250, 343, 351, 353-
    362, 416, 434, 456, 460
Patriot opposition, 298, 346
Pelham family, 1cc, 158, 562
Pelham, Henry
    death, 66j
    estates, 1aa, 38, 66j, 66q-r,
        101

letters from and to, 1a, 1e, 2h-
l, 8, 11, 16, 18, 20, 23, 30,
40, 43, 47, 48, 50, 53, 64,
66a-s, 67, 68, 73, 77, 80-
83, 89, 91, 93-96, 98, 100,
102-104, 106, 109, 110,
113, 115-117, 119, 124,
125, 128-130, 133, 137,
139, 142, 146, 147, 151-
154, 160, 162-164, 166,
169-172, 174, 179, 183,
184, 186-193
Paymaster accounts, 89
town house, 107, 560
Treasurer of Chamber
accounts, 101
Pelham, Henry, of Stanmer, 1x,
101
Pelham, Thomas, 1st Baron
Pelham, 1x, 101, 328
Pelham, Thomas, of Stanmer, 1x
Pelham-Holles, Henrietta,
Duchess of Newcastle, 1v, 32,
57, 66p, 66r, 329, 549
Pelham-Holles, Thomas, Duke of
Newcastle
family correspondence, 1a, 1v-
x, 24, 53, 57, 64, 66p, 66r,
144
final audience with George III,
4
final illness and death, 1x, 562
honors, 1u
library, 126
obituaries, 3
personal and household expenses, 1y-z, 66q, 101
property records, 1y-z, 31, 35,
38, 57, 66q-r, 101, 170
Pengally, Sir Thomas, 104, 149
Percival, John, 1st Earl of
Egmont, 208
Percival, John, 2nd Earl of

Egmont, 47, 438
Pitt, J., 66g
Pitt, William, 1st Earl of
Chatham, 58, 66d, 66p-q, 67,
69, 188, 190, 191, 349, 350,
437, 498-500, 593
Pocock, Sir George, 132
Polwarth, Lord, *see* Hume-
Campbell
Portland, Countess and Duke of,
see Bentinck
Post Office, 393
Potts, H. 66h
Press, The, 372, 376, 377, 437,
443, 452
Pulteney, William, 1st Earl of
Bath, 5, 66a

Reade, Henry, 66q
Reay, Baron, *see* Mackay
Regency Council, 73
Reynolds, Richard, 87
Richmond, Duke of, *see* Lennox
Ridley, Mr., 66g
Roberts, John, 66, 66g, 66j, 532,
534
Robinson, Sir Thomas, 1st Earl of
Grantham, 20, 59, 66b, 66e-f
Robinson, Sir Thomas, 115
Rochford, Earl of, *see* Zulestein
Rockingham, Marquis of, *see*
Watson-Wentworth
Rothes, Earl of, *see* Leslie
Rowley, Sir William, 165
Royal family, 1d, 1m
Royston, Lord, *see* Yorke
Russell, John, 4th Duke of
Bedford, 66b, 66e, 78, 79,
183, 358, 520
Rutland, Duke of, *see* Manners
Ryder, Sir Dudley, 66f, 66k, 115,
116

Sackville, Charles, Lord Middlesex, 66a

Sackville, Lionel, 1st Duke of Dorset, 66k, 148, 151, 152

St. Clair, James, 136

Sandwich, Earl of, *see* Montagu

Satires, 115, 252, 253, 258, 260-262, 266, 276, 279-282, 289, 292

Schaw, Gideon, 118

Scotland, 1t, 66j, 66-l-o, 74, 93, 366, 368, 369

Scrope, J., 66b

Secker, Thomas, 465

Selwyn, J., 80

Seven Years War, 196

Seymour, Charles, 6th Duke of Somerset, 83

Seymour, Edward, 8th Duke of Somerset, 83

Shackleton, John, 527, 532-534

Sharpe, John, 127

Shelvocke, George, 66h

Sherlock, Thomas, 185

Shirley, William, 117, 129

Skinner, Brinley, 44

Sloane, Sir Hans, 63

Smollet, Tobias, 547

Somerset, Duke of, *see* Seymour

South America, 97, 479, 489, 490

South Sea Company, 1r, 22, 116, 406

Spencer, Charles, 3rd Earl of Sunderland, 53

Stair, Earl of, *see* Dalrymple

Stanhope, Philip, 4th Earl of Chesterfield, 66d, 66k, 139, 180

Stanhope, William, 1st Earl of Harrington, 56, 66d, 66h, 66k, 133, 153

State Papers Domestic, 73, 74

State Papers Foreign, 75

Steele, Sir Richard, 149, 171, 251, 333

Stepney, George, 16

Stone, Andrew, 50, 66a-b, 66e-h, 66p

Stone, George, 66k, 115, 194

Stuart, John, 3rd Earl of Bute, 40, 98, 193, 225, 229, 439, 440, 451, 453, 521

Suffolk, Countess of, *see* Howard

Sunderland, Earl of, *see* Spencer

Sussex politics, 1x, 1bb, 342

Sutherland, Earl of, *see* Gordon

Tabuerniga, Marquis de, 66g-h

Tankerville, Earl of, *see* Bennett

Taxation and finance, 1j-l, 1n, 12, 60, 66b, 66d, 66g, 378-386, 441-443, 445, 503-507

Titley, Walter, 36

Todd, Anthony, 69

Tonson, Jacob, 146

Tories, 563-575

Townshend, Charles, 2nd Viscount Townshend, 339

Townshend, Charles, 3rd Viscount Townshend, 66h, 143, 155

Townshend, Hon. Charles, 104, 118, 143, 144

Townshend, George, 4th Viscount Townshend, 124, 143

Trade, 2a, 406, 441, 486-489

Treasury, 76, 382-384, 505-507

Trelawny, Col., 66h

Trelawny, Edward, 113

Trentham, Lord, 66h

Trevor, John, 3rd Baron Trevor, 53

Trevor, Robert, 1st Viscount Hampden and 4th Baron Trevor, 142, 162

Tucker, John, 103

Tudor, Jos., 66m-o
Turner, Thomas, 224
Tweeddale, Marquis of, *see* Hay
Tyrawly, Baron, *see* O'Hara

Vanbrugh, Sir John, 205, 329,
   p. 113
Verelst, Harman, 125
Vernon, Edward, 42, 97

Wade, George, 66-l, 91, 95, 103
Waldegrave, James, 1st Earl
   Waldegrave, 82
Waldegrave, James, 2nd Earl
   Waldegrave, 50, 218
Waldegrave, Sir William, 120
Wallmoden, Amalie, Countess of
   Yarmouth, 58, 66b, 66p
Walpole, Horace, 4th Earl of
   Orford, 202-204
Walpole, Horatio, 1st Baron
   Walpole, 39, 49, 56, 66a-b,
   66d-e, 90, 137, 179, 185,
   408, 412
Walpole, Sir Robert, 1st Earl of
   Orford, 66b, 80, 115, 122,
   335-337, 414
War Office, 73, 77
Warren, Sir Peter, 9, 117
Watson-Wentworth, Charles, 2nd
   Marquis of Rockingham, 109,
   195, 231, 454, 455, 457

Wentworth, J., 66c, 66-l
Wentworth, Thomas, 40, 115
West, James, 37, 66b, 66k

West, Richard, 140
West Indies, 1r, 37, 66a, 89, 113,
   480, 492, 493
Westmoreland, Earl of, *see* Fane
Weston, Edward, 153
Whigs, 563-575
White, John, 1c, 199
Whitefoord, Allan, 66-l
Whitworth, Charles, 39, 166
Wilkes, John, 27
William Augustus, Prince, *see*
   Cumberland
Williams, Sir Charles Hanbury,
   66b, 66e, 66g, 100, 135
Wilmot, Sir John Eardley, 7
Wilmot, Sir Robert, 142, 143,
   161
Winnington, Thomas, 209
Woods, William, 66g
Wyndham, Charles, 2nd Earl of
   Egremont, 27

Yarmouth, Countess of, *see*
   Wallmoden
Yorke, Charles, 2c
Yorke, Philip, 1st Earl of Hardwicke, 2a, 2h, 2m, 34, 66a-b,
   66e-f, 66h, 66j, 66p, 115,
   172, 173, 196, 217, 569
Yorke, Philip, Lord Royston and
   2nd Earl of Hardwicke, 2b,
   2k, 2o-p, 213

Zulestein de Nassau, William, 4th
   Earl of Rochford, 66g, 104

About the Author

P. J. KULISHECK is a lecturer in history at the University of Minnesota, Minneapolis. She became interested in the Pelham brothers while doing research for her doctoral dissertation.